For the Outsider

For the Outsider

Poems Inspired by H. P. Lovecraft

Edited by S. T. Joshi

Hippocampus Press

New York

Published by Hippocampus Press
P.O. Box 641, New York, NY 10156.
www.hippocampuspress.com

Cover art and design by Daniel V. Sauer, dansauerdesign.com
Hippocampus Press logo designed by Anastasia Damianakos.

First Edition
1 3 5 7 9 8 6 4 2

ISBN: 978-1-61498-413-9 trade paper
ISBN: 978-1-61498-416-0 ebook

Contents

Introduction

The degree to which H. P. Lovecraft and his work have become icons in both popular and high culture can be gauged by the proliferation of poetry seeking to tease out the characteristics that made Lovecraft a distinctive personality and the core elements of his variegated literary output. This volume presents a bountiful array of verse, ranging from pieces composed during his own lifetime by his closest friends to those written in our own day.

As early as his entry into amateur journalism in 1914, Lovecraft exhibited himself as an individual unique in his outlook, his erudition, and his numerous idiosyncrasies. It was not, to be sure, that he deliberately sought to portray himself as an eccentric; but the force of his personality—as an atheist, a devotee of the past, and a delver into the weird and fantastic—was such that those around him took immediate notice. The first known poem devoted to Lovecraft appeared in 1918—an "appreciation" by Arthur Goodenough, a Vermont poet whose familiarity with Lovecraft was drawn only from his work. This naïve versifier's poem contains the grotesque image "Laurels from thy very temples sprout." Lovecraft had thought Goodenough was spoofing him, and their mutual friend W. Paul Cook had difficulty preventing Lovecraft from writing a pungent satirical reply. Later that year, Rheinhart Kleiner became one of the earliest amateur journalists to spend significant time with Lovecraft; his visit with the Rhode Island writer is commemorated in "At Providence in 1918." Kleiner—who became a central member of the Kalem

Club, the informal literary circle that gathered around Lovecraft when the latter moved to New York City in 1924—wrote several other poems addressed to Lovecraft and his wife and to other members of the club; other Kalems, such as Frank Belknap Long and Samuel Loveman, also wrote verse epistles to their friend.

Lovecraft's unexpected death in early 1937—he had kept his fatal illness secret from nearly all his friends and correspondents—generated an outpouring of grief that often expressed itself in poetry. Clark Ashton Smith's elegy "To Howard Phillips Lovecraft" is in its compact way comparable to Shelley's *Adonais* (a poignant tribute to the recently deceased John Keats), evoking not only the man but the essence of his work. August Derleth, Henry Kuttner, Elizabeth Toldridge, Emil Petaja, R. H. Barlow, and many other colleagues paid their respects to Lovecraft in verse. With the passing of years, such poems became something of a tradition; it was fostered by August Derleth, who published many such items in successive volumes of Lovecraftian miscellany under the Arkham House imprint. One of these, "For the Outsider: H. P. Lovecraft," was written by one Charles E. White, about whom virtually nothing is known; but it demonstrates the extent to which even someone who was unacquainted with Lovecraft could be moved to write a poetic acknowledgment of his life and writing.

As Lovecraft's work became increasingly popular and critically acclaimed in the 1980s, a new cadre of poets sought to demonstrate their awareness of the distinctive qualities of Lovecraft's life and character. Veteran poet Brett Rutherford wrote a long elegy that was recited at the fiftieth anniversary of Lovecraft's death at Swan Point Cemetery on March 15, 1987. Two decades later, Leigh Blackmore in distant Australia wrote a similar memorial of the day of Lovecraft's passing. Manuel Pérez-Campos imitated Lovecraft and his friends (who had written acrostic sonnets on the name Edgar Allan Poe in 1936) with an acrostic on Lovecraft's own name.

The pioneering nature of Lovecraft's literary work—tales and poems that explored the insignificance of humanity in a boundless universe—also elicited poetic tributes, or imitations, from an early period. His close friend Alfred Galpin, in "Selenaio-Phantama" (1918), mimicked the verse form of Lovecraft's own poem "Nemesis" only a month after that poem was published. Other colleagues in the pulp fiction world, from Donald Wandrei to Robert E. Howard to Richard Ely Morse, generated poems that sought to capture the key components of Lovecraft's fiction, especially his creation of a constellation of imaginary cities in New England (Arkham, Innsmouth, Dunwich, Kingsport).

In the poems that appeared after Lovecraft's death, several of his narratives appear to have exercised a fascination with poets: the early tale "The Music of Erich Zann," with its fusion of weirdness and music; "The Shadow over Innsmouth" and its portrayal of hybrid monsters from the sea; *At the Mountains of Madness,* that cosmic extravaganza set in Antarctica; and, of course, "The Call of Cthulhu," which introduced the extraterrestrial entity that many have seen as his signature contribution to weird literature (although Lovecraft himself was probably not one of them). Other poets have chosen to treat Lovecraft's themes more broadly—the evocation of "elder beings" who lurk in the shadows; the ambiguous figure of Azathoth, the nuclear chaos; the erudite scholars who pursue forbidden realms of inquiry at their own peril.

What this volume demonstrates most vitally is the broad array of poetic idioms that poets have used to express their inspiration from Lovecraft: metrical verse, free verse; sonnets, quatrains, ballads; Old English alliterative verse, prose poems; rhymed verse, blank verse. Lovecraft himself was a formidable weird poet, although the bulk of his poetry is occasional verse and is oftentimes less than stellar; but generations of poets have used his poetry and his prose as springboards for their own evocative work, and this volume is a tribute to their versatility and insight.

—S. T. Joshi

I. Poems about Lovecraft

Lovecraft—An Appreciation

Arthur Goodenough

Illuﬆrious Lovecraft! Fortune's favored son
With wit, grace, dignity combined in one—
Entranced we linger while thy ﬆrain conveys
The wit and dignity of earlier days.

Men told us dully Poetry was dead
And Nymph and Dryad from the foreﬆ fled,
But hither summonsed by an Orphic ﬆrain
Their former haunts are populous again.

Scarce since the days of Michael Angelo
Did such prodigious induﬆry have show;
And even as with that immortal One
Nothing thou doeﬆ that is illy done.

Who would deny thee bays? I make no doubt
That laurels from thy very temple sprout;
The printed page that makes us weep—or laugh
Conveys more meaning than a photograph!

Like a magician holding in his band
His single tool the wonder-working wand,
Thou calleﬆ up Aﬆarte and her doves
And ancient revels waken in the groves.

Oft has the flow of thy delightful rhyme
        Charmed with the skill of less prosaic times;
And like the rod of Aaron has thy pen
    Blossomed in beauty for the eye of men!

Happy the man who not too soon is born,
        And not too late beholds his natal morn;
Whose star no baleful influence obscures
    And every Oracle success assures!

Accept this tribute to thy sterling worth,
        May Heaven find thee 'ere thou leavest earth!
Accept this tribute to thy genius! Nay,
    Decline it not—it is a debt we pay!

Greeting

John Milton Samples

To H. P. Lovecraft, Esq.
(A Reply)

Whene'er throughout the smiling land
The Silver Clarion's notes are heard,
The touch of Lovecraft's master hand
Shall sound in song and rhythmic word.

At Providence in 1918

Rheinhart Kleiner

I left my own Manhattan, seeking pleasure,
    And having journeyed hence
A hundred miles, I found it in full measure
    In teeming Providence!
I sought her hidden ways and quaint old places
    That neѕtled ev'rywhere,
And found that Time had left benignant traces
    On alley, ѕtreet, and square!
I thought of one for whom these ways had beauty
    And splendour all their own:
My friend, whose path of pleasure and of duty
    These scenes had only known.
And over all the cloud of war hung drearly;
    The summons to the ѕtrife
Was soon to come; and one whom I held dearly
    Was near the close of life!
But with unclouded brow and heart uplifted,
    All unaware, among
These scenes and sights, by golden summer gifted,
    I mov'd—for I was young.

To Satan

Samuel Loveman

To H. P. L.

"Tu tires ton pardon de l'éternal martyre,
Infligé sans relâche aux coeurs ambitieux."
—*BAUDELAIRE.*

When, mid the hyacinth deep that girds the sky,
You saw, O Brother, ere your eyes grew dim,
In wrath and loneliness the sight of Him,
Amid His bow'd and litten hierarchy:
Heard songs that fell from lips half-strange with years,
Outcast and ruin'd, beautiful in flame,
You—with the lost among the damned few,
The fallen rebel crew—
Hearing the flattery that fawned His name,
Turn'd back to hell a face that shone with tears.

Did you not at the sunken portals wait,
And where the golden estuaries fell,
Gazing at heav'n before the glow of hell,
Stretch forth your hand to where the tyrant sate?
With the first cry that shook th' enslaved world,
Swift, silver, clarion, Lo! I make you free,
Free as the winds and as the waters are,
Sons of the morning-star!
O souls of mine, I give you liberty—
No withering hate into the darkness hurl'd!

Not from those spaces charm'd to dusk and rose,
    Nor in the scarves with light and music pent,
    Came the soft wail of disillusionment,
But lower than the lowliest in their woes,
The trodden and the dispossess'd of fate;
    These, brooding in a quiet flash of tears,
        By stars that to the massive night are graven,
        Recall'd their austere haven
    The sorrow and the bitterness of years,
Conceiv'd in ruin and embalm'd in hate!

And now shall men no longer fear and dread!
    For heav'n is shattered, faded is the host,
    That without pity judg'd the tortur'd lost,
And radiantly parcell'd forth the dead.
See! where your molten throne uprears in night
    The legions gleam, the drowsy vultures wing;
        That which first met your plaintive, human eyes,
        Ev'n that, is paradise. . . .
    At last, my Brother, the awakening!
Ere dawn appears, a perfect chrysolite.

Epistle to Mr. and Mrs. Lovecraft

Rheinhart Kleiner

(Imitated from Mr. Pope)

My Friends, though Phoebus held the lyre,
And play'd with true, celestial fire,
While, close around, the Heav'nly Nine,
Applauded ev'ry strain divine,—
Yet could not he, whom Loves imbue,
Contrive a fitting song for you!

Alone, did each of you possess
More Worth, than Bard might well express;
Together, your Desert is such,
That none could sound your Praise too much!
No Panegyric, then, shall be
The Motive of these lines from me!

But I shall hope that wedded years
May strengthen all that now endears;
That Venus, with as kind an air,
May guard your Love from Doubt and Care;
And Hymen ever linger nigh
To trim the Torch still burning high!

May Truth and Beauty walk beside,
To warn, to counsel, and to guide;
And Faith and Hope, as well, to keep
Your footsteps t'ward the tow'ring steep,
Upon whose Summit rests the Crown
Of endless Honour and Renown!

Bacchanale

Samuel Loveman

(To H. P. Lovecraft)

A flagon is filled for the vintage guest,
    The grapes are crushed at the brim;
The young lord loosens his loric vest,
Violets bound on his brow and breast—
    And the revel is all for him,
  The revel is all for him.

There, where the orchards fire and smoulder,
    Agavè dances around;
Arm to white arm and shoulder to shoulder,
Naked Pentheus leaps to enfold her—
    But the Mænads make no sound,
  The Mænads make no sound.

In Mysia, a low wind shakes and sighs,
    An oarsman calls to his crew;
There is a cry the dead man cries,
Once, ere the darkness fills his eyes—
    With a knife that his mother drew,
    A knife that his mother drew.

The Four of Us!
(Rondeau)

Rheinhart Kleiner

The four of us forsake the street
For this aloof and calm retreat,
And rest us from the cares of day
That fly, while fresher fancies play
Around us where the hours are fleet!
How sad that Time's unwearied feet
Should hurry most when life is sweet
And we have much to do and say,
            The four of us!

How often, brothers, shall we meet
With hearts that still serenely beat?
How many years are ours to stay
With minds as cloudless and as gay?
May days to come but kindly greet
            The four of us!

The Double "R" Coffee House,
Feb. 15, 1925

PRESENT:
    H. P. Lovecraft
    S. Loveman
    G. Kirk

[To Lewis Theobald]

Frank Belknap Long

Hail Theobaldus, Prince of Singing Sires*
Whose Blakean vision thrives on Wrenish† spires
Whose flaming genius soars from Pope to Poe
And on old Mather's pages, row on row
Descants, whose lucid wisdom shames the Stars
Whose love of learning shakes our Prison Bars
And shows us worlds unknown, O Lewis Hail!
May every future quest attain the Grail!

*grandsires
†Christopher Wren, an *obscure* English architect (1632–1723)

To Mr. Theobald

Samuel Loveman

(*Upon His Return to Providence*)

In Providence at fringèd eve
Old Theobald takes his cap and cane,
And where the antique shadows weave,
Dreams his Colonial dreams again.

Sees the pale periwigs that pass
Pause delicately by, then fare
Past balustrades that shine like glass
To seek his eighteenth century there.

Dream, Theobald—close your tired eyes,
Forget the ruder world around;
Only these by-gone folks were wise,
Only the vanquish'd world was sound.

Hold them an instant if you will,
Shadows of perfume, light and flowers—
We never knew their grace until
You, by your genius, made them ours!

After a Decade

Rheinhart Kleiner

Dear George, I stood dreaming a moment today,
Where once your old bookshop enlivened the way.
The house of decrepit and shabby red brick,
Whose stoop was all cracked, and whose locks would not click,
Has added a decade of dust and despair
To decades already deposited there.

What matter? I thought of the room where the boys
Once came to partake of your fireside joys;
Where lyrics and laughter were frequently heard,
And poets to prosers were greatly preferred;
Where you, genial George, watched the glass or the cup,
Ever prompt in presenting or filling it up.

I thought of the boys—for as boys they appeared,
Though some by old Time had already been sheared;
Of Sam and of Howard, of Arthur and Vrest—
And some who have wandered to East or to West;
Of "Tal" and young Belknap, of James and old "Mac"—
And some whom no summons can ever call back.

But mostly I thought of the one in whose mirth
The brightest and best of our moments found birth:
The skeptic, who beamed with the kindliest cheer;
The cynic, who wanted his friends ever near;
The host, always ready to serve and to do—
In other words, George, I was thinking of you.

Elegy: In Providence the Spring . . .

August Derleth

For Howard Phillips Lovecraft

Howard, has spring come down the college yard
paﬆ sixty-six to Swan Point now? (no number has the heart,
the spirit has no place but in the mind that knows
the memory.)

                    Here in the country, March blows
down the sky, south wind abroad, and spring in the air:
deep in the ponds frogs ﬆir to warmth, tall clouds are fair
on ice-freed water. Ah, how many times the heart leapt up
at redwings' song, the early hyla's cry, the arum's hooded cup!

You knew them years before; together now they tell me
you are gone: wind's cry in every thickening tree,
owl's mourning down the slopes of air, the lone
hawk's scream—these echo grief where ﬆone
and willow leaf invite the sun. Ah, how bitterly all earth and sky,
—wind, trees, brook's sound—cry
out at Death: one touch returned to clay
your animate flesh! No more a day
to bring your letter, no more the brilliant fancy, no more
the guiding counsel, the warmth of friendship on the page:
            and yet—beyond the door
ﬆill Cthulhu walks, the Arab cons his Necronomicon,
the deathless Ancient Ones shine on!

Howard, how fares the vernal season now in Providence,
how down the wooded lanes, the field beyond the fence,
there where your footsteps passed, where still the leaves of autumn
        and the dust
lie scattered where you walked? There is no world for grief so deep;
        I must
believe what heart rejects: dust to dust, and even you gone
        the long mile
to death: but the heart keeps faith, the mind holds tight to you,
cannot but hold you all the while
that time allots this flesh.

        Howard, the stars wheel over now
    as always, and spring comes down to swell the bough
where now you lie: (the heart un-numbered, the spirit's place in
memory): past sixty-six, down lanes and streets so bare of you,
the spring comes down to Swan Point now . . .

25 March 1937

To Howard Phillips Lovecraft

Clark Ashton Smith

Lover of hills and fields and towns antique,
How hast thou wandered hence
On ways not found before,
Beyond the dawnward spires of Providence?
Hast thou gone forth to seek
Some older bourn than these—
Some Arkham of the prime and central wizardries?
Or, with familiar felidae,
Dost now some new and secret wood explore,
A little past the senses' farther wall—
Where spring and sunset charm the eternal path
From Earth to ether in dimensions nemoral?
Or has the Silver Key
Opened perchance for thee
Wonders and dreams and worlds ulterior?
Hast thou gone home to Ulthar or to Pnath?
Has the high king who reigns in dim Kadath
Called back his courtly, sage ambassador?
Or darkling Cthulhu sent
The sign which makes thee now a councilor
Within that foundered fortress of the deep
Where the Old Ones stir in sleep
Till mighty temblors shake their slumbering continent?

* * *

Lo! in this little interim of days
How far thy feet are sped
Upon the fabulous and mooted ways
Where walk the mythic dead!
For us the grief, for us the mystery. . . .
And yet thou art not gone
Nor given wholly unto dream and dust:
For, even upon
This lonely western hill of Averoigne
Thy flesh had never visited,
I meet some wise and sentient wraith of thee,
Some undeparting presence, gracious and august.
More luminous for thee the vernal grass,
More magically dark the Druid stone,
And in the mind thou art forever shown
As in a magic glass;
And from the spirit's page thy runes can never pass.

For H. P. Lovecraft

Henry Kuttner

The pain is a little less now
    For a wound may heal with time,
But because of a wound that may never quite heal
  I make this rhyme.

Not with a sure and skilful hand
    But because of a word you said,
I have tried to count the world's loss
  Now you are dead.

And the world's loss is a great loss,
    With fame at the long road's end,
But the world knew you through your words:
  You were my friend.

And the flame of art shall be brighter
    For the strange fire you lend,
And many shall mourn the Titan:
  I mourn my friend.

April 1937

H. P. Lovecraft

Elizabeth Toldridge

He calls us not (as modern craftsmen do)
    To scenes attained, where sin's hideous scars
On human souls are gilded—no—but to
    The far, pure, foamy galaxies of stars!
Terrors he brings and things not known before,
    From lone and dismal haunts of old dead suns.
Yet are our spirits outward-drawn—to soar
    Through vastnesses where a stainless Wonder runs!

Divinity

To H. P. L.

Elizabeth Toldridge

It is your mind that is of kin to me.
    Yet, of the mind, some make a thing but borne
    Of juggling forces, atoms blent or torn
Apart—electrons, whirling dizzily!
You look at me with eyes that seem to see
    The dreams of all the ages men have worn
    So proudly; eyes that pity the forlorn,
That cannot hide your spirit, strong and free.
And so I hug my simple faith. I know
    My needs great answer lies within my reach:
        A light that shines in darkness all the while . . . .
Nothing evolved from nothingness could show
    Such splendours as are hinted in your speech,
        Such glories as are shadowed in your smile.

Yet Still We Mourn

Frank Earle Schermerhorn

(Dedicated to the Memory of Howard Phillips Lovecraft)

Why has he crossed the barrier,
This friend that we had made?
Must he go on, though we may not,
To Plato's classic shade?
We know that silence now has stilled
For us his kindly voice;
His learning, all his mystery,
News passed out earthly choice
Some hidden, palmed oasis-land
Has called him far away:
Some desert blooms again unseen
Where he has gone to stay.
Those ancient glories that he dreamt
Have come to him, reborn;
Their magic visions glow for him. . . .
He lives—yet still we mourn.

H. P. L.

Henry Kuttner

Here in the silent places, and the caverns beneath the world,
On the great black altars carven from the stones that the gods have hurled,
Where the gray smoke coils and shudders through the eery purple gleam,
And the shadows of worlds beyond our worlds fall over a dreamer's dream—
Reddened with blood from an alien flesh, pallid as vampire thing,
Dark with the glimpse of supernal night and brushed with an ebon wing,
Pageants of awful majesty pass in a saraband
Like the shadows of Egypt's Titan gods far-flung on the changeless sand.

Only a few may taste the cup that none but the gods can drain;
Valhalla is lost to the stolid throng of the peaceful and warm and sane;
Evil, they say, is the lonely night where it is not good to be,
Chilled with the cold that is more than cold, paying the dreamer's fee,
Resting on couches of asphodel, resting and wonder-drowned,
Ageless and lost to a humdrum world, with magic and glory crowned,
Facing the gates of the universe, breasting the mighty stream
That bursts from the roots of Yggdrasil, in the splendor of a dream.

Lost Dream

Emil Petaja

To H. P. Lovecraft

Exalted, whose far-off visions see
In memory's mist a land of whispered dreams
Where beings god-like move in shadowed schemes,
A silver city by a sapphire sea.
They work their spells, and plan when they will be
Among the mystic dancers, under beams
Of crystal crescent moons whose radiance seems
A light or necromantic sorcery.

I gaze enchanted while they pass me by;
Ascend the hill where crumbling ruins lie—
An eery sea-deep sound rings out the moor;
They pause before a rock which hides a door:
One fumbles in his scarlet cloak. I see
His slender fingers move—he turns a key.

H. P. L.

Albert Chapin

Unbounded was his range of information,
The logic of a literary might,
Whose thoughts refreshed, like dew on vegetation;
Colloquial, his powers that gave delight.
To him a gift meant joy that came with giving
A bridle-path along sweet wisdom's way.
The voice has gone—but deep in mem'ry living;
His written page the gods have doomed to stay.
No more is he to scan or judge our "posies,"
A tangled mass no husbandman would spare;
From seedling thoughts he cultured lovely roses
And left his lonely blossoms drooping there.

H. P. Lovecraft

Frank Belknap Long

The many now who see in you a glass
    Held steadily against the outer dark,
Where Memphian shadows throng, and glories pass,
    Illumined by the Eternal's fitful spark,
Glimpse but one facet of a wondrous light
    That fell miraculously on Earth's harsh shores,
And shed a radiance on the Spirit's flight,
    That turned the priests of Mammon from our doors.

To the high mountain peaks your vision soared;
    Across the glacial green which links the world
Of splendid dreaming with the night's unfurled,
    And eon-wide pinions by the blind abhorred.
Sublimer beauty never dwelt with Poe,
    Or walked with Shelley in the white dawn's glow.

H. P. L.

R. H. Barlow

I. March 1937

There is engrained in us the twisted myth
Which, using as symbol the change from worm to wings
Or slain year's birth ensuing eager springs,
Makes parables to silence weeping with.
Since it distracts the empty hand of grief,
I set the scentless blossom in my soil
And seek to mend with slow uneager toil
The ravaged plot, the broken stem and leaf,

And know I shall not fail, though wandering far
To see the gulf which bounds my yesterday.
Since Sorrow's word must hastily be drowned . . .
They prate of Somewhere, call you highly crowned
With Christian wreathes throughout eternal day.
You, who are crowned with Death's tremendous star!

[March 1937]

II. March 1938

And now a year recedes into the wash
Of aimless centuries, and now my eyes
Perceive the pattern of their fall and rise,
Yet memories are the heart's incessant lash
Like rain upon the cloudy ocean hurled.

All paſt and future hours emerge as one—
Twin ſtars which swing about a perished sun
In some far reach of night beyond the world.

What thing makes gulls defy the pushing breeze
Or iris bloom, what knife of silver flame
Was bright in you, a year can scarcely tame.
It flares up yet beyond the shipless seas.
But I upon this beach, perplexed by night,
Dare not advance bereft of your keen sight.

[March 1938]

[Untitled]

The ocean vaſt from myriad darts of rain,
The seeds of atoms sprouting into ſtars,
The cells of flesh, its ecſtasies and pain,
These things are one, masked by its avatars.
That comets whirl, that sinew clings to bone,
That seedlings swell, that inseɛts spawn and die,
Is fore-ordained—the patterned evening sky
Is brother to the patterned river-ſtone.

Prolific life spills out of chance's cup
Across this lawn of green and golden fields,
The fountainous grain matures and thereon yields
To mouths of drought, but other crops well up.
In this design all cosmic patterns blend,
Involved and gorgeous, void of ultimate end.

[1938]

[Untitled]

The night of iron, the day of foam is made,
And though brief worlds in briefer ages spin
Round hot-eyed suns, their anthracitic kin
Dead stars of the abyss, will see displayed
In time Death's signal . . . all sieged lands
Whose armies break, must scar the cherished wall
With final wound, and signify its fall
With some black banner held in reluctant hands.

Though various dust shall of his flesh be spun
And eddied off when this dear jewel Earth
Is once more hid with kindred star and sun
In rayless vaults, the gods with maddened mirth
Have wrought them Man, to laugh and dream by day,
Ignorant of night, till it sweep all away.

[1938]

H. P. L.

The dimensionless sun, an hour since white with flame
    Withdraws its beams from glades grown dusky green,
    Silence walks from fastholds scarcely seen
By birds or eyes of furtive woodland game.
The phlox afire beneath this blossoming sky
    Is stirred by wandering winds in sudden hush
    Van Gogh set down with gaudy narrative brush
Such hues and patterns sifted through his eye.

As yesterday, the pines are tall and dark
        And meaningless against the yellow glare,
        As yesterday, the eyes of twilight stare
Confirming naught, the sunlight's tired spark
        Departs; and eastward move the glooms
        Where Sprague Memorial dominates the tombs.

I took a room in Providence at the Y
        Since Mrs. Gamwell wished to be alone:
        A decent place, though somewhat lacking tone,
And had my breakfast—prunes and toasted rye,
In dripping butter steeped, and paid the dime
        Knowing you liked the fare and would not come
        Again, and that your active flesh was some
Way off, and still for what remains of Time.

I saw such things as you had liked to see—
        The evening sunset radiant from the hill—
        Sorting your papers before the dust was still.
Since you could not, the task remained for me.
        Going to the washroom with toothbrush, towel, and cup,
        A Goddamn fairy tried to pick me up.

On such a night the high majestic moon
        Seems less removed, as wreathed in flimsy robes
        Her body bares among the stellar globes
Each minted bright as some engraved dubloon.

The evening shares the delicate pretense
        Of kindliness which nature has assumed,
        As captive woman, claiming passion doomed,
To torment more, from adamance relents.

They thus deceive; the blossoms and the stars,
        Beguiling us into a perfumed snare;
        And if chance aspects force the mouth to swear
The galaxy as more than aimless spars
        Adrift; to join by night such graceful play
        Is not amiss, since it departs by day.

[March 1939]

H. P. L.

March 15, 1940

I shall write until the wind is done scraping the air
That my brain is two brains,
And one is dead,
But the other is alive in the
Clutched clay fist,
A frog with painted muscles.

I shall write of death with selected words,
Of the lilies killed with the shadow
Of the four sides of death
Still lacking your initials;
Of the flooding voice running over stone tears.
The rose I took is in a box
Or dropped out of the book I gave Catherine,

Whether Mrs. Gamwell has kept the house
I don't know;
The road being greyer even than your inn,
I have pulled my horse's head from it,
Forever.

March

With sombre pen the icy rain
Has drawn a scrawling line to stain
Spring's document, begun so plain.

The woman Wind, with love congealed
To hatred, walks the blighted field
Divested of its half-grown yield.

Impartial through the world the sleet
Treads blossoms down beneath his feet;
While from a window moist with heat—

Content in a security
No falser than belongs to me—
My warm cat bends his neck to see,

And seeing, soon will drowse again,
Heedless of the blossoms slain
To halt the hunger of the rain.

[Spring 1938]

H. P. L.

Rheinhart Kleiner

You sit among us when we pour the wine
And read the lyric or intone the song,
When melody and mirth the hours prolong,
And talk is fervent, and our faces shine;
Shedding a glory or a spell benign
Among the fancies that about us throng,
Your presence seems as certain and as strong
As if your voice had called, or you had made a sign!
We speak of you and what you felt or thought;
We quote you as we might some friend away,
And chuckle at some foible all your own;
So vividly and variously you wrought
Your magic in our pliant hearts, that they
Hold warm a name now chiseled on a stone.

For Howard Phillips Lovecraft

Robert A. W. Lowndes

The pathos of a great moth, beautiful
    Crushed by the world's fanatic cruelty,
Drawn ever onward by the mystical,
    Eternal light of unknown fantasy.

To Howard Phillips Lovecraft

Henry George Weiss

Master-writer of the weird, essayist, poet, 1890–1937

He lived—and now is dead beyond all knowing
Of life and death: the vast and formless scheme
Behind the face of nature ever showing
Has swallowed up the dreamer and the dream.
But brief the hour he had upon the stream
Of timeless time from past to future flowing
To lift his sail and catch the luminous gleam
Of stars that marked his coming and his going
Before he vanished; yet the brilliant wake
His passing left is vivid on the tide
And for the countless centuries will abide;
The genius that no death can ever take
Crown him immortal, though a man has died.

For the Outsider: H. P. Lovecraft

Charles E. White

My sleep has been uneasy since he died.
There have been tappings on my windowpane;
where nights were still before, voices have cried,
I have heard whisperings in grey autumn rain.

I have ransacked the tomes of frightful lore
for easing of a dark, unhallowed dread
that, nightlong, saw him lost, outside a door,
with broken key . . . mocked by the eyeless dead.
In spectral watches of wan winter nights,
I have wrenched my eyes from doom-lit caves
where flame-eyed wizards plagued him with stark blights,
and tortured demons screamed from heated graves.

Then, on a night when flesh could bear no more
of half-guessed horror, I took up that key
(You know it well. *He* left it!) to the door
the shoggoths guard through black eternity.
Seven monstrous gates swung, soundless, shut behind.
Time, space, the dark dimensions were as one
soul-shattering projection of *his* mind
who broods forever in a nameless sun.

All the dim secrets those watched roads could tell
They Who Hold Power sponged from my waking brain,
save this thing only: there was a gold-tongued bell.

Wide rivers of light welled out across a plain
where turquoise towers sheered from crystal walls,
and he stood waiting, smiling at the din
of strange laughter pealing from moon-drenched halls.
There was a door swung wide to let him in.

No echoings will jar my sleep tonight,
No bat-winged things will scour the countryside.
There will be no black fears that shun the light,
Now that the lonely one is safe . . . inside.

In Memoriam: H. P. Lovecraft

Richard Ely Morse

Arkham and Innsmouth knew his questing tread
And kingdoms lying lost beneath the seas,
Within his keeping were the fabulous keys
To gates of aeons where his spirit fled;
From alien days a veilèd figure led
Through monstrous lands and primal dreams that freeze
Even the Elders in their mysteries;
He braved them all—and now men call him dead.

Perchance he told too much, and so strange wings
Agleam with all the colour out of space,
Beat down one night and carried him afar
To join the pageant of those tragic kings
Ruling the future of an unknown race—
Immortal daemons of a dying star.

Anniversary

R. H. Barlow

I cannot sleep. The rising wind of years
        Through memory sifting, lifting the leaf's
        Brittle anatomy, blows together griefs
Of child and man, and wakened memory hears
Howard's voice above the desperate toss
        Of branch, and memory sees the god inlaid
        With brass bugs abandoned where we stayed
Some childhood year, leaving a sense of loss.

And thou, Vincente, legend-wealthy heir
        Of Teotihuacán mid shepherd folk,
Chilled with the stone mask the princes wear
        By the simple word a line of lightning spoke!
Nothing we love is given us to keep.
The wind of years is rising. I cannot sleep.

[15 March 1947]

HPL

Vincent Starrett

He didn't wait for his laurel wreath,
　　He couldn't stop for the long applause:
Someone called from a distant heath
　　With urgent news of an ancient cause,
　　And he slipped away in the poignant pause
Between two strokes of a midnight bell . . .
　　I think they met him with proud hurrahs
Who led him down to the gates of Hell.

And there were they who had gone before,
　　To crush his fingers and speak his name,
At the cheerful Inn of the Creaking Door
　　With its ringing glasses and hearth aflame.
　　Edgar . . . Louis . . . and Arthur . . . Fame
Dubbed him Howard and hailed him peer.
　　We who cherish a meaner claim
Well may spare him a facile cheer.

Homage to H. P. Lovecraft

Felix Stefanile

The young boy watched, as the sun on the bay
turned honey streaks, (and where the gulls flew past
the sunset flickered), how the closing day
drew, in its wake, the small skiff of the moon

that sailed up the slate sky: the clouds, like waves,
formed silent blasts that blew across his mind
a stinging spray, from airy seas, till far
he heard a clanging in the wind away.

He dreamed himself a mariner in Space,
one with those Indians, or Arthur, who
in their sad, burning boats, flamed toward the sky,
to wake and read their fate in the moon's face.

A lonely boy, without a sail to spy
in the long land, he dreamed of distant seas,
and the wide, ivory home of the silent moon.
The stars were rich as wine in their star-froth,

and as he dreamed, he felt a velvet tug
at his thin sleeves, and looked about,
and saw beyond all fear and wonder, that he stood
not by the bedroom window, but in a Court

where Arthur, helmeted and sad and gray,
standing before him, formed slow words to hear:

"Now you are come to us," the old king said,
"you must know we have waited long for you

to sing our losses, though you cannot stay."
Rewards and plenties were in the boy's gaze.
There he spied Pontiac, and Billy the Kid,
reckless Orlando, and those dreadful twins

Faustus and Merlin, of whom he had read.
He could not yet believe that he was dead.
"Tell me," he started. Arthur said, "I will,"
and bending low, he whispered. Like the wind

that riffles through the trees, his words fell forth,
till the young lad was drunk, as on star-froth.
In the clear fields bells sounded, rising slow
as tinkle of first foxes in that land

of the owl's bush, where toad, tree, stream and moonlight
whispered strange words, and like a horn, the sea
called out his war to him. Then he awoke.
His mother wondered that he seemed so pale.

"Go out and play," she said; "it's a bright day."
He thought of Mordred, and the sea-shell south,
the seven busy sins, and the falling sun.
Of time his presence, he was lost to time,

dreaming of a rich wreckage on the moon.
The night came, Mordred, and his word ran wild:
there is a lucky kingdom we shall lose:
King Agony will win the bony plain.

H. P. L.

Clark Ashton Smith

Outside the time-dimension, and outside
The ever-changing spheres and shifting spaces—
Though the mad planet and its wrangling races
This moment be destroyed—he shall abide
And on immortal quests and errands ride
In cryptic service to the Kings of Pnath,
Herald or spy, on the many-spangled path
With gulfs below, with muffled gods for guide.

Some echo of his voice, some vanished word
Follows the light with equal speed, and spans
The star-set limits of the universe,
Returning and returning, to be heard
When all the present worlds and spheres disperse,
In other Spicas, other Aldebarans.

Lines to H. P. Lovecraft

Joseph Payne Brennan

You read the cryptic sorceries of night;
Across the whirling gulfs of eldritch space
You traveled on a wizard's spectral flight
To wake the dreaded Elders in their dreaming place
And wrest from wary Guardians of the Gate
A runic lore that banished godheads keep.
The acolytes of silent Ib pursued too late
For you were safe beyond the wall of sleep.
Among the haunted stars your legends grow—
Who fathomed secrets nameless demons know!

Revenants

August Derleth

By owl's light, bat-flight,
in the small hours of the night
I start awake to fearful sound . . .

What trembles underground
far down, down deep
on the perimeter of sleep ?
What shuddering ululation rises but half-clear?
to tempt the outward-straining ear ?
Who calls upon the Ancient Ones indifferent to man's race?—
Shub-Niggurath, Cthulhu with the face
Of tentacles, Nyarlathotep, Azathoth—who wait
forever on the rim of time and space.

        The hour is late
for human kind; in R'lyeh's deeps
Great Cthulhu sleeps,
and Hastur lurks beyond the Hyades.

What moves across the stars, just past the trees?
What monstrous shadow lengthens tangibly
beneath the moon?
            Howard, this is your legacy.

A Walk in Providence

J. Vernon Shea

The sunlit ways on golden afternoons
Attract the hikers and the Sunday brush;
But witches gambol under darkling moons
On lonely moors while all the world's ahush.

In Providence its favored son set out
To view the fanlighted and leaded doors,
The rank, sea-crusted ancient wharves, no doubt
Still haunted by the cries of murdered whores.

A bat flew past, a gaunt from out the night,
And hooting owls did mock and match his pace.
A caterwauling thing gave him a fright
When, stooping down, he saw it had no face.

To H. P. Lovecraft

S. T. Joshi

Death consoles:
You would not care to see
What men have done with your name;
Your work; your spirit; your tardy fame.
You would not care to see
This battered earth, with grinning apes
Whose acts no surprise would cause,
But pain.
Yet you were a cynick:
And Reason found a home—
In both your heart and mind?
Or were you some quaint mystic
Whose foe "Reality" was?
Again:
Were you artist or exorcist?
A gibbering fiend whose true home
Was that empty cell at Sefton?
God! what little minds
Have preyed upon that chipped
Yet awesome monolith of your work!
Without your vision they
Durst pull you down,
That you could cease to gaze upon the stars
And taste the mind that fills *their* mouths and minds.

They would hack and peck;
Remould those runes etched in blood;
For of what other triumphs can they speak?
Giggle in your grave:
And watch these ants on this grain of sand
Smother your page with slimy ichor.
What care you? Your task is done:
You have lit a darkness that now can never dim;
Have built an edifice of marble and gold;
Of porphyry and lapis lazuli
Whose lustre defies alike
The worm and the night.

At Lovecraft's Grave

On the Fiftieth Anniversary of Lovecraft's Death March 15, 1987

Brett Rutherford

1

That does not sleep
which can eternal lie,
yet Howard, Old Gent, Ech-Pi-El,
Lovecraft who signed himself
Grandpa and Theobaldus
to his fans and correspondents
most assuredly sleeps here.
We drift into the vale of earth,
the gentle falls and slopes
of Swan Point Cemetery,
gather to remember and praise him
as the Seekonk with its silted memories
ribbons at the edge of vision.
The sculpted monuments
        of angels and Psyches
repeat the largesse
        of immortal promises
not so for his simple stone
placed forty years too late
to help his absent-minded shade
come home.
                Yews and cedars

bluff Ides of March
with bitter green, droop branches
like soiled wigs, while honest
bare branches of an oak tree
retell the long years' chase of sun,
the repeated losses of winter.
Which is the emblem of Lovecraft's sleep?
His life lies stripped
as that sorrowed oak
where his initials are carved
(real or spurious?)
his nightmares the evergreens,
        lingering through seasons,
harboring nightwing
    as readily as lark.

2

We stand about, a handful
swelling to nearly a hundred,
trying to envision his folded hands,
his hand-me-down Victorian suit,
wonder how much of his habiliments
have fed the indiscriminate hunger
        of the conqueror worm,
his eye sockets empty and dry
        gone beyond dreaming
though we close ours and see
the tower of ageless Kadath,
the shark-infested ruins of Ponape,

the imaginal Providence
where he walked arm-in-arm
with Poe and his eccentric Helen.

Our Lovecraft, lord
of the midnight shudder,
eaten from within
by the gnawing shoggoth of poverty,
the Azathoth of squamous cancer,
the loneliness of Nyarlathotep,
drugged by nurses into the sleep
where dreaded night-gaunts fly
and bent flutes warble
a twisted melody

and yet he faced it stoically
        like a proud Roman,
        an 18th century gentleman.
Death came with burning eye
and found him not trembling,
never recanting his cosmic vision,
waving away the white-collared cleric
        with a wan smile.

3
Hundreds of miles we came today
to pause and pay homage,
readers and scholars who have leafed
his books, studied his papers,
debated his sources and meanings,

traced his footsteps in Gotham
and Boston and Federal Hill,
stood with a thrill
    at his one-time door.

In sorry, mean-spirited Providence
no plaque or marker reminds us of him.
His grandfather's estate an empty lot,
his mother's house vanished,
his last abode uprooted and moved
like an aimless chessman on street map,
as though the upright town
        with its sky-piercing steeples,
        mind-numbing priests,
would like to erase him.

A baby in mother's arms
intrudes on our reminiscing,
breaks Carl Johnson's eulogy
with gurgles and cries of
"R'lyeh! Wah! R'lyeh!"
(shunned name of the city of doom
where multi-tentacled Cthulhu
dictates his madhouse symphonies!)

As Joshi reads sonnet
        the sun blinks off
behind a humped shoulder
        of cloud,
and the air turns cold,

unnaturally cold
in a spell of seconds.
Earth reels beneath our feet
into the chasm of sunless
space.

4
Ah! this is the moon's business,
or the work of a moonless night.
Should we not speak of him
beneath the glimmer of Hyades,
the velvet pall of the void,
the primal ether in which the cosmos
whirls like a raft into maelstrom,
the vast interior spaces
of Time and the Angles
where the gods as he knew them
drool and chant?
But they will not permit us
to assemble by night.
They seal the gates
against our ghoulish
intrusions,
pretend that the coffined dead
cannot be heard
to turn in their neglected
crypts, deny
that lingering essences
drawn from the memories

of the living can take
    an evanescent life

pale shadows of shadows,
        reflected gleams
from the dusty pane
        of a mausoleum,
glints from polished granite
        or marble,
a sliver of sourceless light
in the eye of an owl
    or a raven;

pretend we are not
        untuned yet powerful
        receivers of thought,
    transformers of vision,

as if we did not know
how night
        vibrates with poetry,
        eidolons plucked
from the minds of the dead.

Reporters and camera crews
take us in warily,
eye us for vampire teeth,
        chainsaws, machetes,
        jewelry and witches' teats,
wonder what crimes we lust

beneath disguises
to perpetrate
upon their babies,
their wives,
their altars.
We smile,
keeping our secret of secrets,
how we are the gentle ones,
how terror
is our tightrope over life, how we alone
can comprehend
the smile behind the skull.

5

Later a golden moon lifts up,
swollen with age and memories,
passing the veined tree skyline,
leaving its double in Seekonk,
disc face scanning the city—
the antfarm of students on Thayer,
the tumult of traffic on Main,
the aimless stroll of dreamers,
dim lamps of insomniacs,
the empty, quiet graveyard
winking like a fellow conspirator
at the prince of night.
Dimly on obelisk
a third moon rises.
The offered flowers

against the headstone
quiver and part.

A teenaged boy,
backpack heavy
with horror books,
leaps over the wall,
eludes the sleepy
          patrol car,
comes to the grave,

hands shaking
frightened,
exultant,
hitch-hiked all day

waiting,
mouthing the words
of *Necronomicon,*
for a sign
that does not come
the clear night,
the giant moon
throbbing
as he chants:

That is not dead
which can eternal lie,
And with strange eons
even Death may die.

Providence: March 15, 1937

Leigh Blackmore

Into the ward where, lying weak and still,
A pallid-featured man looks hollow-eyed
Upon the door, there comes with deathly stride
A silent, hooded figure. "If you will . . ."
Intones the spectre, taking Lovecraft's arm,
"It's time to seek what lies beyond this room."
The man gets up. "Surely you've come too soon?"
But, "Where to now?" he asks, his manner calm.

"Perchance you will," the visitor exclaims,
"Enter the realm of Chaos, vast and blind,
And groping through the gloom fatefully find
The aeon-old black book of daemons' names;
Will open it to see—mad truth of Hell—
In your own hand the letters: H P L!"

In a Sequestered Churchyard Where Once Lovecraft Walked

Leigh Blackmore

Dim past and present meld on College Hill.
Its houses brood, o'ertopped by verdant trees
Whose susurration fills me with unease;
Might gaslight's glow illume this place e'en still?
Here dreams the churchyard where vast elm trees grow.
One senses here the shades of writers passed;
One bows one's head in coming here at last,
Where Lovecraft's spectre pays *hommage* to Poe.

What honour walking where his footsteps fell,
Sensing with friends (and whisp'ring in hushed tones)
The spell of state-house dome, cathedral-bell,
Centuried ghosts amidst the hoary stones.
Mysterious truth this hidden churchyard gives—
In Providence today, Lovecraft yet lives!

In Swan Point Cemetery

Robert H. Waugh

At last I have assurance. His bones lie
to disarticulate beneath this stone
and looser lie. His earth accepts its own
unearthed decomposition casually,
flesh of our flesh, but makes us recompense;
all dissolution operates the bleak
engine that runs the year and does not break,
bees stop our mouths in gold from Providence.

His better part he leaves to our disputes,
a sublimate, odd prolegomena
against the seawind blustering in tonight;
till anonymities in grey-striped suits,
nothing new-fangled for them, enter, weigh
and bear us off to place us to his right.

Ave Augustissime: An Acrostic Sonnet on H. P. Lovecraft, Esq.

Manuel Pérez–Campos

How is it that thy handshake seems as if
press'd by one ris'n to haunt, and not long dead?
Lucid scribe of Angell St., thine each line's a riff
on ghoul'd drifts, thine each missive's Yrs for a dread
viﬆa of ﬆarr'd gulfs that gyre without a plan.
Enrob'd entangler of tombs who, by wick-flame
crimp'd by unclos'd sills, evokes the rot of
rogue aeons with non-Euclidean élan:
Allow by dint of this thine encoded name—
fungi-dreamt—for us, cowl'd here at Innsmouth's cove,
to glimpse thee by some olde gate's miﬆ again.
Enravish'd by thy warp'd imagin'd voice,
ﬆill we luﬆ for more, that we may learn to ken
quaintly—and, in our own cursedness, rejoice.

On a Threadbare Photograph of H. P. L. at 66 College St.

Manuel Pérez–Campos

As the tourmaline rhythms of the Milky
Way dwarf the spirit & the First Baptist
church campanile, you (a revenant in
an old-fashion'd suit whose art of
ventriloquizing the lucifugous festival
of infinity has been dreamt under
the auspices of Urania) stand steadfast
by your porch as if some ethereal extension
of Britannia & wonder, as your hunger
prospers, when is it that the night-gaunts
shall come again? O in your hazel eyes
I can hear you oppress'd by the thought
of voids beyond the sidewalk under your shoes
& beyond the clouds over your fedora.

H. P. L.: R.I.P.

Manuel Arenas

Beyond the Wall of Sleep, in atramentous bardo
Shuddersome scenes replay, ever in eldritch tableau.
May Eve at Meadow Hill, cultists chant their baleful song
"Iä! Shub-Niggurath! Black Goat with a Thousand Young!"
Innsmouth maids, lain with frogs, breed an amphibian race
Hominine until time shows their Demi-Deep-One face.
Richard Upton Pickman, with aberrant ghoulish flair,
Paints his nightmare visions ensconced in his North End lair.
At the dark libraries of the Miskatonic U.
The *Necronomicon,* grave, is laid away from view.
In dim, sunken R'lyeh, the Great Old Ones dissemble:
Constrained Cthulhu bides to surge as dreamers tremble
Whilst direful Outer Gods in unlit space are scheming.
In his grave at Swan Point, dead E'ch Pi-El waits dreaming.

Seer of Black Spheres
(for H. P. L.)

Scott J. Couturier

Throw open squamous cellars of the soul!
Beauty & dread in consummate measure—
bard of black planets that in anguish roll,
vision solely illuming their nether.
Utmoſt pleasure in Void's adumbration:
in far-flung fantasy blisses abound.
Yet, also fear's all-acute elation—
gnosis 'mid bright Abysses without bound.
Seer of sightless viſtas & loathsome height,
Kadath's pale pilgrim, a-wandering ſtill:
thunderer who evoked the awesome might
of Powers older than name, yet with Will.

Weaver of Wonders, dark scion of Awe:
Revelation reigns where madness is Law.

The Haunter of College Hill

David Barker

He strides up Benefit and then down Church,
Past old St. John's where rows of headstones lean.
Long after midnight, not a soul is seen;
Odd shadows quiver and then seem to lurch.
Vile lunar beams illuminate the way.
Ecstatic Poe once frequented these lanes,
Cool air upon his neck, a moon that wanes,
Reminding him of her who would dismay.

Alone, this walker wanders till first light.
Few men are brave enough to follow suit.
The thought of things unholy in the gloom
Excite his mind to realms of vivid fright.
Soon echoes of clawed feet in hot pursuit—
Queued up, a crew of corpses portend doom.

Lovecraft

Fred Phillips

A gruesome daze, in midst of routine day
As rare as worlds beyond our mortal sight
Endures despite what any choose to say
In every soul that bides the fall of night.
Of aeons past he shewed what spectres reigned
O'er mortal haunts from far beyond our ken.
Forbear, ye of this sphere, to ponder more
Of what our feeble race hath brought to light.
The universe, as boundless as before
Distinguishes what cleaves our day from night.
Those who remain to witness must recall
The reason we endure on Earth at all.

II. Poems Inspired by Lovecraft

Selenaio–Phantasma

Alfred Galpin

Dedicated to the Author of "Nemesis"

In Elysium-fann'd fields of my slumber,
In the wild-tinted beauties of night,
I have feasted on sights without number,
Recreated all Heav'n with my sight:
And I wake to the sunrise at dawning, fit close to the dusk's mad delight.

Shadow'd visions of beauties unpainted,
Shifting sights of a Heaven beyond,
Primal nature in pureness untainted,
Without Man and his slave-making wand,
Meet my sight in procession uncanny, unorder'd, and link'd without bond.

Mingling phantoms above Man's poor notion,
Phantasmas obscure and unknown,
Undulations and waves of wild motion
Into infinite variance grown,
I behold in my slumbers of madness, from far shores of mad Cynthia blown.

I have seen things of cryptical meaning,
Hinting life far above mortal view;
Superstitions of primitive gleaning
Blend with fancy to forms strange and new;

And my fetterless brain leaps the mountain of Science and dreams ’tis
not true.

All the hopes of a life are entwined
With the greed of a fancy unchain’d,
While my thoughts, by the sleep undermined,
Wander wordless, uncheck’d, uncontain’d
O’er unearthly expanses of Spiritland, haunting where once they had
reign’d.

When, in midst of this immundane dreaming
Come effulgent the first rays of light,
Bringing back my rapt soul with their beaming,
Lending splendour to all within sight;
And I wake to the sunrise at dawning, fit close to the dusk’s mad delight.

The Unknown Color

Donald Wandrei

Whence came that unknown color? Was its source
Beyond the violet, within the red?
Impalpable, a brain-shaped thing of dread,
A glowing form, it drifted on a course
Malefic, purposive, with alien force
That followed through the chamber where I fled.
I found no door, and when all hope lay dead
I tried to scream but heard no sound, no hoarse,
Despairing cry. I crouched against the wall
In that dark chamber, numb with terror, mute,
Nowhere to flee, however I might strive,
The unknown color hostile in pursuit
That swiftly toward me now began to fall,
A sentient entity from hell, *alive.*

Arkham

Robert E. Howard

Drowsy and dull with age the houses blink
    On aimless streets the rat-gnawed years forget—
But what inhuman figures leer and slink
    Down the old alleys when the moon has set?

Mad Dream

Richard Ely Morse

(for H. P. Lovecraft)

Here is an alien land, where mountains reach
In shapes accursèd to a shrouded sky;
Darkness is shattered by one wailing cry,
And waves fall evilly upon a beach
Of tittering sands; no warnings need to teach
Benighted travellers that 'tis beﬆ to lie
Far from that town where hooded figures fly
Above the rooftrees, mouthing each to each.

In noxious ecﬆasies the houses lean
By ﬆreets that tangle in a shifting flow
Of shadow, and no man had better know
The gate within the maze of vaults obscene,
Where aeon-tunnelled angles draw him down
To face the blasphemy of that dead frown.

Shadow over Innsmouth

Virginia Anderson

(Dedicated to H. P. Lovecraft by Nanek)

We have forgotten some of mankind's ways:
The art of dying, or say . . . Mercy's gift.
So when age grows upon us and our days
By span of man are numbered, the seas rift
And take us in. Then in the rites of old
We pledge allegiance where the strange pale gold
Of obscene Gods dispense eternal life
Wherein to glory, savour and renew. . . .
Free from the world's alarms and strife
In ocean palaces of coralous hue,
Shedding the shape of man and doubling back
In form at least on evolution's track.

The Acolytes

Lilith Lorraine

The Elder Ones are stirring as the red
Stallions of chaos champ their bits with rage;
And they have sent their messengers ahead
Proud with the knowledge of their alienage.

They walk apart from men, the Acolytes,
By stagnant pools and rotting sepulchers,
Whispering of dark, delirious delights,
As young gods die among their worshippers.

They dream of dim dimensions where the towers
Of Yuggoth pierce the decomposing dome
Of skies where dead stars float like evil flowers
Afloat on tideless seas of poisoned foam.

Black tapers glow on many a ruined shrine,
The patterns coalesce—the good, the bad—
The old familiar stars no longer shine—
And I—and I—am curiously glad.

Mountains of Madness

Richard L. Tierney

Grim ranks of frozen spires rear high to face
The world like walls that guard far lands of dream—
White, ivory fangs whose jagged summits seem
To lance the skies and pierce the fringe of space.
No life survives in that Antarctic clime,
And yet the demon wind that pipes and shrieks
Among those spires is like a voice that speaks
Of evil things in accents old as time.

No man has seen beyond that range of snow
The vast black city sprawling grim and cold,
Yet dreamers speak of monstrous things of old
That ooze through vaulted corridors below,
While some have warned of what may rise again
From the black gulfs to face the world of men.

To Great Cthulhu

Richard L. Tierney

The moonlight strikes the waves with waning shafts,
Making a million eyes wink evilly
From undulating facets of the sea,
While landward curls a thickening mist that wafts
Vague scents that bend the dreams of sleeping men
Down nightmare paths bypassing space and time—
To primal fanes that rise from layered slime
Where dreams the One who waits to rise again.

O mighty Dreamer!—when the impending stars
Shall make to rise from out the haunted sea
Thine age-encrusted throne, and cause anew
Thine awful hate to wake and the old scars
Of Earth to burst asunder, grant to me
The vengeance tendered to thy chosen few!

In Memoriam Arthur Jermyn

Ann K. Schwader

Not all life's hidden horrors lie between
Unhallowed depths of space & hollowed earth:
Humanity itself holds much unseen
That's better so; yet brooding toward some birth
Through science into hard, unblinking light.
Self-knowledge beckons, but that adder's kiss
Secretes a lethal venom banned by right
Of sanity to memory's abyss.

The merest mirror glimpses may suggest
Some denizen of daemon-ruins lost
Beneath the Congo's dark unquiet breast . . .
What price self-knowledge now? What fearful cost?
So simple slivered glass may prove a curtain
Cruel as spider silk, & as uncertain.

After Lovecraft's "Facts concerning the Late
Arthur Jermyn and His Family"

The Coming of Chaos

Ann K. Schwader

None dare to speak of it, & few suspect
That shadow-claws clutch inward day by day
(Too subtle for man's science to detect)
Upon this world still wobbling on its way
Between dim pasts in which it played no part,
& grimmer futures gnawing at its heart.

Our hierophants of physics little know
Dread Chaos bears a nearly human face:
Lean as the East where nighted rivers flow,
Yet lightless as that nether void of space
Where muffled drums & tuneless pipers laud
The mad gyrations of an idiot god.

This deity alone does Chaos serve
As lying herald & as messenger
Whose lightest word speaks nightmare down the nerve
Of all who hear . . . and hearing, might prefer
Their ignorance new-polished & pristine
To hinted knowledge twisting toward obscene.

Fresh shrieks of horror haunt the urban night,
Dreamstalked by darkside visions of some end
Crouched formless, nameless till the stars spin right,
Then shatter from the pattern they portend
Of tortured oceans spattered to the sky
By that which should not live, but would not die.

Thus reason treats with madness to survive,
& knowing skirts the borders of unknown
As Terra's erstwhile masters now alive
Deny whatever dust they claimed to own,
But—being mortal—merely held in trust
For Others who esteem them less than dust.

Inspired by Lovecraft's "Nyarlathotep"

Dunwich Pastoral

Wade German

Your inherited thoughts,
like deformed birds
twittering in a fog
that clouds your brain.

You ignore the shadow of
demented offspring
at the upper window,
the toad-throated voice

and gibberish song
that drove you outside,
nerves now whittled down
to inbred bones.

The stones of the well
are cool to the touch;
the soft black water soothes,
unclots your head.

As the mist begins to lift
from the blasted heath,
you settle like a leaf
on needful deeds,

hearing the swaying pines
in still night air,

the rumblings from the hill,
the ground below.

Faint Echoes

Ann K. Schwader

(Pyramid of the Moon, Moche)

Within these ruined walls, an ocean lies,
Though no such ocean as the earth has known.
Both bright & dark at once, its art defies
All expectation of what may be shown
& what must not, for sanity's own sake,
Reveal itself to any mind awake.

Grim lord of all this mythic painted sea,
One figure out of nightmare dominates.
His alien gaze repeating endlessly,
Enwreathed by tentacles, suggests the fate
Of captives as an octopus's prey:
Exsanguinated, slaughtered, tossed away.

Yet such zoomorphic rationales cannot
Eradicate the whisper of a fear
Forged by atrocities our world forgot
Before the first ape stood—yet drifting clear
As corpse-scent through this dim miasmal air,
An echoing of madness & despair.

What drove the Moche priests to draw their knives
Across the frantic pulse of human throats,
To fill their chalices & drink the lives

Of men like sacrificial sheep or goats?
Ancestral memory . . . ancestral dreams . . .
& deeper still, a deathless Dreamer's schemes.

Inhuman, mutter archaeologists,
Not fathoming the truth behind their words:
Star-spawned survivals veiled by legend's mists
& rituals which mercifully obscured
Their origins with horrors too mundane
To seed suspicion in a scholar's brain.

Within these ruined walls, an ocean waits
In token of that ocean set with stars
Though dark between them as this planet's fate
When His black city rises from some far
Abyssal exile to proclaim its place
As mortuary temple to our race.

> "After all, the strangest and maddest of myths are often merely symbols or allegories based upon truth . . ."
>
> —H. P. Lovecraft, "The Shadow over Innsmouth"

“The Hound”

W. H. Pugmire

I hear your ceaseless cry in tortured ear
As fate solidifies before my eye.
This Holland hill will be my moonlit bier
On which my mangled corpse will putrefy.
My breastbone is the bed of your icon,
Your amulet composed of antique jade;
That emblem formed in forgotten aeon,
That distant age of which you are one shade.
Ah, Sphinx of Hell, your grin is ever-wide,
It is the final doom I gaze upon.
No paltry god can stall my homicide,
No poetry from *Necronomicon.*
I take your savage kiss into my heart
As trenchant recompense for arcane art.

“The Outsider”

W. H. Pugmire

Oh, you are but a distant memory,
A phantom in some mental corridor,
A spectral and elusive visitor
I might have known in time of infancy.
Did you, in childhood’s hour, caress my head
And silence childhood’s agony and gloom;
Or hold me in some dank and dim-lit room
Where, wretchedly, I dwelt among the dead?
I call for you within in the lonesome place,
Although I cannot recollect your name.
I stagger ’neath black trees, confused and lame,
And try to catch in memory your face.
Perhaps you rest within the heap of bone
To which I stumble, dazed and doomed, alone.

The Keeper of the Innsmouth Light

M. F. Webb

Across abysmal waters, cursed and restless,
My light keeps its wan faith with hope to rescue
Sailors lost and foundered near this shore,
But interrupted in its constant turning
By our black reef and creatures countless teeming,
It shines instead on sundry fearsome rites.

My nightly torments issue from those rites,
Nightmares deep and mad and keening restless,
Racked by glimpses caught of monsters teeming.
Like sailors lost, for me there is no rescue,
Only Dagon's threat and monstrous turning,
Only fearsome hybrids on this shore.

'Twas Obed Marsh brought nightmares to our shore,
The priests presiding o'er those cursed rites
Of every Halloween and May-Eve turning,
The lights and chants and figures diving restless
That came with industry and promised rescue
And left a town with sickly promise teeming

That fated night when Innsmouth's cursed teeming
Ended the revolt upon its shore,
My father's death, his hopelessness of rescue,
Left me lonely to defy the rites,
To hide myself from priests and creatures restless
And Dagon dire in his abyssal turning.

And now with every year and season turning,
His words recalled of horrors endless teeming,
I pace the lighthouse nightly doomed and restless,
Knowing I must keep my watch to shore,
For strangers chancing on accursed rites
Would find but vile shades, no hope of rescue.

Obed claimed he brought hence Innsmouth's rescue
But from my point I watch the townfolk turning,
Denizens corrupted by their rites,
The priests, their diadems with menace teeming.
Here there is no reassuring shore
Only secrets mad and cruel and restless.

Death, my rescue, calls—and I am restless
For its turning, rescue from this shore,
Doomed Innsmouth teeming, falling to its rites.

Kiosk to Kadath

Chad Hensley

When frail night's veil has completely entwined
My thin form, wrapping a shroud of sleep tight
An ancient kiosk appears in my mind.
Its dark center churns inhaling all light
Spiraling inward I am sucked in too,
Hurling through an infinite outer space
To land before a gate of silver hue.
Far beyond reach from any mortal race,
Shrill cacophonies howl in stellar wind;
Through labyrinthine avenues I wander
In darkness inhuman to comprehend.
Feeling oddly alien I ponder
These monstrous dreams consuming me each night
Stretching my tendrils awake with delight.

Zann

Ian Futter

It squeals and screeches
through the void;
ebullient screams,
and howls of joy.

His fingers fast,
on fretted boards,
twist from their joints
to chaos chords.

Strained notes through unknown octaves
spin
from resined bow
of cryptic skin,

an ancient air,
thrust through the years,
away from vapid, feeble ears.

Faster, faster
plays the fool.
The instrument with human tool.

Vast window,
open to the night,
like hungry maw,
receives his rite.

Forty Years in Innsmouth

M. F. Webb

To live as lighthouse wife—some called it doom;
A future once enormous bound, then shrinking,
But I loved him enough to brave the chill
To trade the busy square for sky and ocean.
'Twere secret then to me the shoreline rites
And Obed Marsh's love of things abhorred.

Away from town and farm, those priests abhorred
Were distant shapes that threatened secret doom,
And if my friends and kin engaged those rites,
I did not know, my past relations shrinking.
To me, their absence was a greater chill
Than any spawned near monstrous sky or ocean.

Then loneliness gave way to greater chill
As his obsession swelled with the abhorred,
Dull hours spent with a spyglass trained on ocean,
Determined to preserve the lost from doom.
He could not see his greater purpose shrinking
As in his way he fell prey to their rites.

I cannot say if these were devil rites,
Although their crazed abandon struck a chill
Which shuddered through my soul and left me shrinking.
Perhaps 'twas just their strangeness I abhorred,
The unfamiliar chants portending downfall

The priests and supplicants beside the ocean.

Till years of tending beacons by the ocean,
Protecting foundered ships from demon rites,
Convinced me that we two faced certain doom
If only from past neighbors now turned chill,
As we ourselves became the ones abhorred,
The safety of our lighthouse dimmed and shrinking.

And seeing all my hope and promise shrinking
I resolved to flee far from the ocean
Far from all my husband now abhorred.
I begged of him to disregard the rites,
To seek a warmer clime, forswear the chill—
Yet still he ruminates on others' doom.

I—rather than embrace impending doom
From land or ocean dark entombed and chill,
Our past abhorred—have left him to his rites.

Azathoth

Charles Lovecraft

A dream's malignant locus in my head
Foretold the end of all things known. The talk
On loud, annoying radios, would squawk
In horrible sound bytes. My dead ears bled,
Filling with suppuration my bleared mind,
As if some marsh had leaked its filthy damp
Into the chasms of my being, black swamp
That I could never shake from its dark bind.

But Azathoth had come some said, and prayed
To all their gods, and the whole Earth grew hot
Like some mad magnifier burned our spot
From realms beyond all time, and source betrayed.
    Atomic chaos seared all life like some
    Summer of love—save that its love was doom.

R'lyeh

F. J. Bergmann

Dreaming, an ancient entity twitches in its sleep,
Sleeps deep beneath the veils of age and dust.
Dust falls in silence in the Eldest House.
Housed in stone like a brain within a skull,
Skulking in the passages of thought,
Thoughtless, near-insensate—yet it lives,
Lives upon lives in universe after universe,
Versed in rituals transcending space and time.
Time for the conjunction of the darker stars,
Stars come right at last for Cthulhu, dreaming.

The Crypt of Nitocris

David Barker

Inspired by H. P. Lovecraft's "Under the Pyramids"

At Giza on the midnight sands,
I fell into fierce Bedouin hands.
A perilous drop by spooling rope
into a realm devoid of hope.

In chambers far below the Sphinx—
a woman's torso with head of lynx.
Of flesh, not marble, she was formed
in heaps of gore where beetles swarmed.

And hybrid mummies of King Khephren—
one half, hippopotami; the other half, men.
Parading through expansive rooms
more likely used as homes than tombs.

Then monstrous progeny, quite obscene,
foul issue of the ghoulish queen.
Offering praise with dusted breath,
to an Unknown God of Death.

Oh, countless wonders that blaspheme,
or was it all but fevered dream?

Elder Beings

Leigh Blackmore

They came across abysses from doomed planes
Unutterably distant, far from ken
Of human beings writhing in their pain
Of mortal life—mere women and mere men.

They fled their crumbling towers and citadels
In search of living planets for their use
And so Alhazred's secret mad book tells
They flocked and settled on the Earth, let loose

To rave and raven. Human minds succumbed
To alien thought-forms of these Elder Things.
Through fevered dreams their dreadful visions thrummed,
These creatures with their terrible black wings.

And so at last it was that humankind
Obliterated, lived and thrived no more.
The Elder Beings in their might combined
Had shattered human life—so tells the lore!

The Ballad of the de la Poers

Adam Bolivar

The de la Poers in Exham did
    In baron's state once dwell:
A priory whose walls had hid
    A curse from darkest Hell.

The only living de la Poer
    From England swiftly flew,
For all his kith and kin the lore
    Averred he foully slew.

Americans his heirs became,
    Still secretive by trait;
These Delapores were much the same,
    Bequeathed a loathly fate.

Three hundred years had nearly passed,
    When I, the heir, returned,
And Exham was restored at last,
    Which still the peasants spurned.

The memory of folk is long,
    And I was much disdained,
My ancestors reviled in song,
    My reputation stained.

The priory was built upon
    An ancient temple's stone,

Where blood was spilt before the dawn—
A secret now unknown.

Now in my new-built hall I dwelt,
A proper de la Poer,
As had the Saxon and the Celt,
And those who came before.

At night my cat was sorely vexed
By rats within the wall,
Whose passage left me much perplexed,
And led beneath the hall.

When daylight came I searched the vault
With Norrys by my side,
A steadfast friend with little fault,
Who with me would abide.

A Roman temple lay within
Where Atys was adored,
Where rites were held of blackest sin,
And decency deplored.

We slept in there, my friend and I,
To dream of fungous swine;
The rats returned: we heard them fly,
And scratch beneath the shrine.

To London then we hied in haste
To find some learned men,
Who would not shrink when they were faced

With evil in its den.

So seven men then probed the pit
Through Magna Mater's maw,
And afterwards none would admit
The truth of what they saw.

We crept down stone and time-worn stairs
Beneath the Roman tile,
To meet with ape-like skulls' dull stares,
Their cretinism vile.

The twilit grotto from my dream
Was there, my God it was!
We saw in torches' spectral gleam
Bones pocked by rodents' gnaws.

A Saxon house, the swineherd's lair,
Who kept the fungous beasts
In ruins where the noxious air
Still smelt of daemon feasts.

The rats returned to lead me on
To ecstasies of old,
Into the brink, the inky yawn,
Where hunger took ahold.

"I'll learn ye how to gust at me,
At what my kinsmen do . . .
For ev'ry man must eaten be—
Thou stinkards know 'tis true!

“For Magna Mater, Atys’s sake
Agus bas dunach ort!
My herd of swine a feast shall make,
And eat you for their sport.”

They found me then crouched o’er the corpse
Of Norrys, once my friend;
My fiendish face still madness warps,
My freedom at an end.

And all the rats, I hear them still!
They scamper in the walls. . .
Into my bones they bring a chill;
In dreams the swineherd calls.

Shadow over Arkham

Fred Phillips

Wait for me, O stranger; pray do not haste—
Quit me not to thy daemonic strand,
Where milestones of grey torchlight grimly stand
To mark unknown and unseen this drear place.
My lores inform me, where there be a Road
There Beings went before. Do not despair,
Therefore, although the shimmering icy air
Hangs heavy here: the gods will bear your load.

I have believed, as many faithful do,
That what the pallid mortal world maligns
As "phantasy" bears truth of elder kind
That, never stated, none the less is true.
So pray, wait for me: be not faint of heart:
Upon this Road the Source of Wonders start.

The King of Horrors, Howard Phillips Lovecraft

Charles Lovecraft

Start Chant: The King

Quintessence of a mind the dreams that were,
And which race still in that jewelled skull, till age
Itself dissolves, and in his black-eyed stare
An entourage of fears proclaims a sage.

Thus jungles full of paralysing fright,
With haunted visions, twisted scenes he knew,
Are in the horrors always found by night
As the key nourishment that his soul drew.

The Shadow out of Time

Five years a stranger's face the mirror locked
Upon shrewd eyes, and dark things stirred the self.
Invading mind chilled deeply as it mocked.
At last his memory regained its health.
Beneath the deserts of an austral land,
Mid fallen columns, dusts that swirl between,
The willing fool would find *in his own hand*
The writing from the ages he had been!

The Unnamable

Upon the next night there arose in dark,
From long-hushed aisles of tombs where forces free,
A thing that lay on heart its monstrous mark
And cataclysm of what should not be.

Some window panes bear traces of the dead,
Repellent visages that sear the soul.
When those dark forces come to life we dread,
Or worse—we end up chewed and gouged for role.

The Book

Upon the third night I knew rest had gone,
With shaking jewels of beaded sweat that burned
Upon my beetling brow a wedged thorn crown,
And foul, dark meaning of the runes I learned.

I tried to send the book away, but found
That it returned by black uncanny means.
I was to that thing tied and moored and bound,
Through what ill-fated climes and dark demesnes.

The Dunwich Horror

When Wilbur Whateley died he was half-god,
Seed-crossed with monstrous godhead from the blue,
And in his steps a dark divinity trod.
In Dunwich his twin-brother spread and grew.

* * *

That thing got loose and tore the woods apart;
The evil flowed from earth's repugnant maw.
I still see now the trees bent to their heart;
Occultist powders last revealed the awe.

End Chant: Father Lovecraft, Sleep No More

L guides through metaphysic mists that thin,
Revealing callipers of other times;
The circles and dimensions that da Vin-
Ci sings meet in the gong of St. Toad's chimes.

Thus strained by sleeplessness for all drugs' worth,
The wilderness of aeons onward wings;
While from the cosmic planes beyond the earth
The rapture of weird destinies he brings!

Stanzas of the Metaphysical Student Found in a Notebook

Manuel Pérez–Campos

I have come to this squalid holm of misremembering
to study for my exams at the university.
It is an up-piled marginal dank maze of archaic
brownstone: and when it mixes with the imaginary
souvenances required by nightmares it drifts like a vapour
over the rooftops of Paris: notes rayed out by a viol

from a garret spinning under the abyss (a viol
keyed to machine-age angst) annex it to misremembering
though arpeggios that build like an opium vapour
until I misplace where in time is the university
and suspect my desks at dusk there were imaginary
because only those districts of Paris which are archaic

exist—and this garret is anchored in the archaic.
If I should stay within the mannerism of that viol,
and hence opt out of an out there which is imaginary,
I would not have such a need for misremembering
this innhouse courtyard that keeps me from a university
which until fixed on by my psyche must remain a vapour,

nor that bridge which when undertaken renders me a vapour
too, that I may succeed in my flight from the archaic.
Those doctrines I am learning at the university

have helped me counter that feeling directing the viol
of a globe besieged by galaxies: misremembering
the garret from which it hinders the imaginary

is how a Paris addicted to the imaginary
calls me to the defense of factory-billowed vapour
when standing at its belts: it is by misremembering
that the telegraph zeitgeist of scorn for the archaic
turns me from the ether-flumed disclosures of the viol;
and so I seek the colonnades of the university

that I may no longer starve for a university,
having rote-learned the dicta of the imaginary
until I grow wings as its automaton. Though the viol
trill out that one's lifetime is reducible to vapour
and that even Sol's future is doomed to become archaic,
I can pretend all this is false through misremembering.

Let then misremembering be my university.
I sleepwalk past the viol, inured to the archaic:
my maps end in the vapour of the imaginary.

An Apocryphal Addendum to
H. P. Lovecraft's "The Music of Erich Zann"

O Iranon

Charles Lovecraft

Bright Iranon, the gorgeous Aira waits
For your young step to wander cobbled ways,
With gleaming eyes bejewelled with shining haze
And in your beating breast a breath that bates.
O, you were never born for common states,
For you had found the far superior blaze
Of fair dream witcheries, with which to raze
And break the wretched thrall of life's grey gates.

The granite city of Teloth you crossed
With Romnod, and shared years of thoughtless pride,
But at the last you starkly went *inside.*
You stepped into the sands and found the cost,
        Not recognizing dream for what it was,
        A false and gaily painted albatross.

Jenkin

Ross Balcom

The firmament: stars and planets
Run like rats in their courses.

Brown Jenkin has eaten my face.
I must cancel my date with your daughter.

Arkham celebrates the Rodent Mass.
My tail, newly emerged, twitches.

God has eaten His own body.
Say farewell to the Big Cheese.

Brown Jenkin, Brown Jenkin, Brown Jenkin . . .
The universe echoes his name.

Dancing Before Azathoth

Darrell Schweitzer

Came the demon
into the darkness of my dream.
Spake the demon,
"Rise up, take my hand,
and I will show thee
terrors never before imagined,
wonders never described,
secrets never written,
even in the blasphemous tomes of the mad."
So we plunged together into that place
beyond the confines of the grave,
where flesh and bones are sloughed off
and the spirit breaks free to soar.
We waded, stars splashing
about our ankles like foam,
and we dove down to where stone-faced gods
slept and dreamed and waited.
How we fled in terror
from the opening of their eyes!
All stars, all worlds, all dust of creation,
the very tombs of the gods
seemed no more than scum
on the surface of a greater sea,
through which we plummeted now,

in helpless fascination and despair,
until we circled and danced before
the black throne of Azathoth.
From this dream,
neither my prideful, foolish demon,
nor my likewise foolish self,
can ever dare awaken,
lest the lord of that black throne should rise up
and follow us back into the waking world,
and devour it all.

Things Man Was Meant to Know

DJ Tyrer

They didn't want us to know
The investigators and cultists
The true nature of reality
And everything that exists
The cults aimed to hide the truth
Keep secret all its power
The summoning and invocations
The secret of the tower
The investigators did much the same
From the opposite position
Declaring the defence of humanity
To be their sacred mission
The one side plotting vile plans
To bring about our doom
The other side plotting to seal away
The alien god in his tomb
But neither side could comprehend
Neither understood
That these powers and beings were not evil
Nor were they good
But rather they were forces
Like the wind or electricity
Dangerous, yes, but tameable
Biddable to servility

With enlightened attitudes
Great Old Ones became tools
The few who feared or worshipped them
Were recognised as fools
What once was horrifying
Now is commonplace
As alien geometries and minds
Are made to serve the human race
Whether cleanly powering our cities
Or as weapons of war
Or transporting us to other worlds
Through a 'magic' door
Arcane knowledge now is humdrum
A little dull and drear
The human mind merely jaded
Not driven mad by fear
And so it's integrated
Taken as far as it will go
No longer hidden secrets but
Things man was meant to know.

The Sunken City

Ngo Binh Anh Khoa

At last, we'd found the fabled realm of old—
The lost Atlantis, shrouded long in myths.
What earthly findings thence could rival this
Discovery? We thought how we'd behold
The secrets hidden since an Age untold
In any ancient tomes or records; bliss
We felt while heading down the great abyss,
Unfazed by thickening shadows, eager, bold.
But what we saw was not what we'd expected;
The columns looked all wrong, unlike the Greek
Famed architecture, and the walls would leak
Green slime—whose origin could not be detected.
Our submarine traversed the lifeless streets
While we were at the edges of our seats.

The silent hours tensely passed as we
Continued traveling through this darksome place—
A vast, obsidian and cyclopean maze
With weed-strewn streets and strange geometry,
Whose structures seemed impossible to be
And yet they were—in this confounding space,
As though—I mused—some massive alien race
Had built this realm ere it merged with the sea.
More winding roads we passed until we reached
A curious altar with a towering gate

With weird engravings of some unknown weight,
And we, the curious fools, its bindings breached.
From out the yawning maw came things unleashed,
Among which was the wakened Star-Spawned Priest.

Nightmarish were the things that passed the gate
On which our gazes landed, and as fast
Averted, but for some, it was too late;
The spell of madness on them had been cast.
Half of the crew dropped to their knees and shrilled
While clawing at their faces till they bled,
And, within minutes, pallid corpses filled
The ship; each face—contorted—froze in dread.
Although I was among the lucky souls
That managed just in time to look away,
I never shall forget those dreadful glows
Within the eyes that greeted mine that day:
The orbs that eerily shone like acid pools
Upon a tentacled visage drenched in ooze.

The Dreamer and the Dreaded Ones

Frank Coffman

> There is a noise as of a voice
> That calls beneath the sea;
> And all the deep heaves, as in sleep,
> With vague expectancy.
> —From Madison Cawein, "The City of Darkness"

The city not-to-be-named lies there
Far, far beneath the waves,
Most Mankind knows not to beware,
What its horrid Master craves.

He dreams—*though Dead!* And it is said
That from *Deepest Cosmos* come
Great Old Ones from that zone of dread
Seeking Earth, again, as *home*.

They—and their minions—with great yearning
Seek our world, 'though once expelled.
Oh yes! *They* are even now returning
To this place where once they dwelled.

Grim Azathoth, of Chaos the King,
The Outer Gods he rules.
Nyarlathotep, the Terrible,
Pharoah-like who leads Earth's fools:

Benighted Legions of the Lost,
Their senses and wits are dulled,
Not realizing the great cost,
Into dire stupor lulled.

And Yog-Sothoth who keeps the *Gate*—
Who IS the Gate—and knows the way
Back to our realm, where again, with hate
Unquenched, they wend today.

Toad-like Tsathoggua, within his lair
Awaits his prey in sloth.
No need to venture far from there
To leave that fell cave he is loath.

Shub-Niggurath, Black Goat of the Wood,
She with a thousand young.
All those who enter the forest should
Fear her and her myriad sprung.

But don't forget the Dreamer deep,
And sleeping 'neath the tides
The Pacific will *not* forever keep
Dead Cthulhu—who now abides.

The Basalt City

Linn Donlon

Well hidden in the Rub' al-Khali's sands
They say there is a long-forgotten blight
Avoided by the bravest desert bands,
And even when the summer sun burns bright.
Through miles still haunted by a nameless fright,
It is not only dholes that course and kill
Those wanderers who lack sufficient might,
For many-pillared Irem waits there still.

Within the harshest of these lonely lands,
The traveler may see an eerie sight.
Amid the silent dunes a City stands,
On ground too cruel for any mortal wight.
The monolithic gates still stand upright,
Though from the crumbling walls great boulders spill
Of stone so black it swallows up the light,
For many-pillared Irem waits there still.

The temple's doors seem sculpted by the hands
Not of a human but some giant wright,
And after countless years a web of strands
Of silver wraps them still to seal them tight.
The carrion birds that circle sense the plight
Of that which, trapped, yet yearns to eat its fill,
But ages since learned never to alight,

For many-pillared Irem waits there still.

O Prince, who walks this world by dark of night
And bends the younger races to your will,
Your servitors have long since taken flight,
But many-pillared Irem waits there still.

Lovecraftian Visions: A Grander Species of Monster

Andrew White

What if the everything shattered?
What if the sky fell apart?
The random destruction of reason
Would seize the mind and crush the heart.

That is exactly what happened
When Old Ones tore open the sky.
Terror and madness took over
Making it better to die.

Darkness envelops the world
As the human order breaks down.
A grander species of monster
Has risen to take the crown.

And what of the people remaining
Who survived the initial plight?
Abject slaves of the Elders
In a world of endless night.

The Guide

Scott J. Couturier

Down Arkham's mazy streets we wander—
past fanes of dark gods hidden in plain sight.
He smiles at me, & says in a thin, reedy,
excitement-tremulous tone: "Here Nyarlathotep's
avatar came down from the stars to
gorge on the minds of mortal kind."
Gloomy winds moan down an alleyway, detritus
gusting behind a ramshackle, forsaken church:
his eyes gleam like sable marbles as he says,
"We must go in, & leave an offering."

Stumbling over spider-embalmed pews,
towards where a blackened cross curls
inwards in fetal display: we chant wordless
incantations in unison, he instructing me on
pronunciation of some obscene alien diction.
What we leave on that altar I cannot disclose.

"Now," he says, "we go down to the wharves;
to wade into the water, to reach where
the Deep Ones dwell." & I, willingly, follow
the taper of his burning zeal, even as salty
ripples lap around my ankles, wet my waist:
only once he looks back on me, waves breaking
against that pinched, gray mouth as it grins.

"Now we go below; take no breath before."
Beyond that, there is nothing sane to know.

To Curse What the Moon Brings

Maxwell I. Gold

My father hated the moon—and so too did I—not through my own choice, but the curse of some aquatic damnations passed by luminous treachery o'er the years which bled from father to son. The amber glint that sparkled in the dim, hazy glow of the twilight skies begged me to wander along familiar paths near the lake, where the scorn of my father burned deep as the old gods in infinite, undying cities. Every night, the moon sank lower near the burgeoning horizon as black stars hung low, and soft, crinkled whispers of dead leaves crunched beneath my feet unable to fill the silence.

The warm murk of the water shimmered underneath the fat, yellow moon while beast and bane began to murmur within the shrubbery of the muddied, nascent pool whose warnings were never clear to me until now—my father's lunacy never clear to me, until now when spires cracked the surface of the water, their mysterious and ugly eyes ignited by the spectral ambivalence of that horrid moon.

No, it couldn't be.

Soon, the dead leaves were nothing but earthly crumbs as I stepped back, farther from the heinous, bubbling hole of eyes. The sunken city of infinite death revealed by the ageless stars and darkness who slowly were swallowed behind the horizon against the light of the awful, golden moon. Yes, my father truly loathed the moon, and the doom which it wrought upon us, and so too would I —for as long as I live.

Randwulf's Return

Adam Bolivar

Randwulf rode forth   through ravenous darkness
On the back of a beast,   black and wingèd,
Hurling him headlong   into horrors unknown;
The doomed and desperate   dreamer vaulted
From his monstrous mount   into measureless space,
To drift in the depths   of distant stars.
To the weary wanderer   Wóden appeared,
Astride his steed,   the stepper of worlds,
And gave guidance   through the gulf of night.
The dreamer dropped   as dawn arose:
Randwulf arrived in   the refuge of his bed
In a house on a hill,   a hero's return,
A key of silver   clasped in his hand.

Veniat ei Malum qui Vocat Malum

(Let evil come to him who calls evil)

Frank Coffman

The grimoire held such secrets that he craved.
That dark book writ in blood and grimly cloaked
In human skin. Yet he was so depraved
He cared not what his chantings had provoked.
The words leapt from the pages as he scanned
With rowan wand, thinking it would protect
Him from whatever wights this book—long banned—
Were summoned forth. But that desired effect
Of safety—despite the invocation of Hell—
Was hopeless, and his trust had been in vain . . .
For the Thing that answered his well-spoken spell
Brought such stark horror and such surfeit of pain
That his mind dissolved before his body burned.
The wages of the summoner were earned.

Composed between 11 and 12:30 on 2 December 2022

Sentinel Hill

Ann K. Schwader and David C. Kopaska-Merkel

Dunwich deathbed
whippoorwill chorus
of panic

free of the old man's grip
newspaper headlines scream

ink and blood
the same by moonlight
late edition

old house
of cards
danger you can't see

his father's name
the stars reshuffled

a door is shut
the night chorus
starts up again

Azathoth; or, The Daemon–Sultan

Leigh Blackmore

"It is a tale told by an idiot, full of sound and fury,
signifying nothing."—Shakespeare, *Macbeth*

A whining wind drives wraiths of cloud about,
Arousing terror in my nervous soul.
I cannot sleep; the moon is choked; I shout
In darkness direful, black as any coal.

Metallic ghosts are spread upon the lake,
Dim mists that hover, white, opaque and still;
And in my room the air is clogged; I quake,
All veiled and steeped in dark; my flesh is chill.

A candle guttering in darkness here
Seems like my life, so pitiful and small;
Though I am now once more in earthly sphere,
I fear the things that swarm and squirm and crawl.

Abysmal voids have opened to my feet;
Atrocious gulfs have swallowed all my sense;
And though for now returned to my own street
I fear those shifting spaces so immense.

Harsh age had fallen on the ugly world;
Wonder had gone from out the human heart;
Grey cities reared and smoky skies unfurled
Tall towers grim, from beauty set apart.

The shadow of those towers starved our dreams
Of sun and moon and fanciful witch-elms,
The flowering meads of spring and sunlight beams
And visions vast of wondrous cosmic realms.

Rote knowledge stripped the earth of comely wealth
And poets sang no more of golden corn.
They sang of twisted phantoms, of ill-health,
With inward vision bleared and voices worn.

When childish hopes had flown away for good
And all these ills had fallen on the earth
I travelled out of life—I knew I could—
Upon a quest for charms that were in dearth.

It was a quest into the spaces far
Whither the world's bright dreams had flowed and fled.
By day I dwelt and toiled beneath the scar
Of that drear city where I made my bed.

I toiled in shadow; turmoil was my lot
Until the sterile, twilight evening fell.
I knew no groves nor fields in that grey spot—
But just a court wherein the light did well

To penetrate, and windows blind despaired.
From my one casement, nothing but the wall
And shutters could be seen; a lone star glared
When I leaned out, peered far aloft. In thrall

That sole star held me every dreadful night
As I delved deep, absorbed obscure lore

And dreamed much that was bound to fast ignite
The madness in my soul; I did implore

The chaos in my mirror to come forth.
It was the glass of Erich Zann, now mine;
From Rue d'Auseil it came. Both South and North
Had once paid homage to its grim design

And awesome power. Beyond dimensioned space
It offered glimpses strange—black voids alive
With motion and with music—things no face
Beheld without loss of the will to thrive.

Illimitable space! No semblance there
To anything on earth that lives or breathes!
And lost in endless dream I made my prayer
Into the glass, unto the Thing that seethes!

Slow-sailing stars, I knew them all by name
And followed them in fancy when they hid,
Until at length my inner eye became
Accustomed to their secrets; and they bid

Me do dark deeds and formless acts of chance.
Dream-haunted skies swelled down and slowly merged
Within my room's close airs. A dark romance
Of cosmic wonder had me deep submerged—

And then flowed forth the violet midnight streams—
Wild midnight glittering all with dust of gold—

Strange vortices of dusk and fire and dreams
From spaces perfumed . . . over me they rolled!

Now opiate oceans poured into my room—
Sun-litten by weird suns without a name
That lit the space and drove away the gloom
And having in their whirlpools dolphins tame

And sea-nymphs, unrememberably deep.
My body from the window stiffly leaned
As noiseless eddies, space-flown, made me sleep
And whirled and wafted me; it was some fiend

Which had me in its grip and bore me out
For countless days unto the farthest spheres.
I sought the visions men have dreamed about;
Instead, the fiend would show me only fears.

I longed on sunrise shores so green to sleep,
On shores with fragrant lotos-blossoms strewn,
But mindless rhythms drew me to the deep
Of aimless angled space, where to the tune

Of muffled flutes' accursed alien whine
There lives a Thing—a blind idiot God
Created by the cosmos, byzantine,
As joke or jest; and only few have trod

The ways toward this Lord of Mindless Void.
This Chaos Ultimate that gives the lie

To humankind's illusion, now destroyed
Of self-importance. Now, to horrify,

Great Azathoth, a monstrous nuclear force—
Malign, age-old, destructive—holds His sway
Amidst the drums that pulse with rhythm coarse
Played monstrously by paws of grim decay.

I see Him now, as I am whirled apace
Through blackest night; the brilliant stars shine down.
Colossally the foul, aged Chaos Face
Looms large upon my sight; I fear the frown

Of festering dim horrors as they float
About the central void; my soul is chilled
The idiot vortices grow fat and bloat
As yet I tumble; will my life be stilled?

Abomination this! Great Outer Gods!
This Daemon-Sultan on His horrid throne
Gnaws hungry—*live*, despite all mortal odds!
Thin high cracked flutes that make my hearing stone!

Ill-favoured beasts disport around the Thing—
Strange, shapeless, bat-winged, ghastly to behold!
I fall and tumble further as I cling
To sanity's last shreds. Infernal cold!

The sable void and Daemon Azathoth
Fill all my vision as I spin and turn.

Unspeakably abnormal—His dark wrath
Is blasting me; my flesh begins to burn!

Flagitious God, of utter alien source!
No pity there, implacable His reign!
Dark Azathoth, inexorable force!
Can I escape, or shall I go insane?

I whirl anew in this black cosmic heart
That *Necronomicon* once lightly cloaked
With 'Azathoth' as name . . . At last my heart
Beats slow and true; I rue that I evoked

This desperate gambit—ghastly universe!
Damned mayhap though I be, I have escaped
The coruscating *horror* of the curse
Although my sanity is close to raped.

Through space my shattered body does return
To that small room beside the dim white lake
Unspeakably, the life within does burn
But Azathoth my soul has failed to take.

And now, exhausted, fevered, here I lie . . .
To feed the body, just a little broth;
In deep relief, I utter a small cry
Of grief—at having met dread Azathoth!

Sources

Virginia Anderson, "Shadow over Innsmouth," *Acolyte* 1, No. 2 (Winter 1942): 12 (as by "Nanek").

Manuel Arenas, "H. P. L.: R.I.P.," *Spectral Realms* No. 14 (Winter 2021): 19. Reprinted by permission of the author.

Ross Balcom, "Jenkin," *Spectral Realms* No. 13 (Summer 2020): 53. Reprinted by permission of the author.

David Barker, "The Haunter of College Hill," *Spectral Realms* No. 15 (Summer 2021): 79; "The Crypt of Nitocris," *Cyäegha* No. 15 (2016): 44. Reprinted by permission of the author.

R. H. Barlow, "H. P. L.," in H. P. Lovecraft et al., *The Shuttered Room and Other Pieces,* ed. August Derleth (Sauk City, WI: Arkham House, 1959), 206–10; "Anniversary," in *The Shuttered Room and Other Pieces,* 210.

F. J. Bergmann, "R'lyeh," *Spectral Realms* No. 5 (Summer 2016): 95. Reprinted by permission of the author.

Leigh Blackmore, "In a Sequestered Churchyard Where Once Lovecraft Walked," in Blackmore's *Spores from Sharnoth* (Sydney, Australia: P'rea Press, 2008), 18; "Providence: March 15, 1937," in *Spores from Sharnoth,* 19; "Elder Beings," *Spectral Realms* No. 6 (Winter 2017): 72. Reprinted by permission of the author. "Azathoth; or, The Daemon-Sultan." Previously unpublished. Printed by permission of the author.

Adam Bolivar, "The Ballad of the de la Poers," *Spectral Realms* No. 7 (Summer 2017): 70–74. Reprinted by permission of the author.

Joseph Payne Brennan, "Lines to H. P. Lovecraft," *Macabre* No. 5 (Summer 1959): 20.

Albert Chapin, "H. P. L.," *Inklings from Utah* No. 7 (May 1938): [1].

Frank Coffman, "The Dreamer and the Dreaded Ones." Previously unpublished. "Veniat ei Malum qui Vocat Malum." Previously unpublished. Printed by permission of the author.

Scott J. Couturier, "Seer of Black Spheres," *Lovecraftiana: the Magazine of Eldritch Horror* (Walpurgisnacht 2021). Reprinted by permission of the author. "The Guide." Previously unpublished. Printed by permission of the author.

August Derleth, "Elegy: In Providence the Spring . . .," *River* 1, No. 3 (June 1937), 89–90; "Revenants," *Macabre* No. 5 (Summer 1959): 8. Reprinted by permission of the August Derleth Society representing the Estate of August Derleth.

Linn Donlon, "The Basalt City." Previously unpublished. Printed by permission of the author.

Ian Futter, "Zann," *Spectral Realms* No. 3 (Summer 2018): 57. Reprinted by permission of the author.

Alfred Galpin, "Selenaio-Phantasma," *Conservative* 4, No. 1 (July 1918): 3.

Wade German, "Dunwich Pastoral," *Dreams and Nightmares* No. 87 (2010); rpt. in German's *Dreams from a Black Nebula* (New York: Hippocampus Press, 2014). Reprinted by permission of the author.

Maxwell I. Gold, "To Curse What the Moon Brings." Previously unpublished. Printed by permission of the author.

Arthur Goodenough, "Lovecraft—An Appreciation," *Tryout* 4, No. 8 (August 1918): [1–2]; rpt. in Goodenough's "Further Recollections of Amateur Journalism," *Vagrant* [Spring 1927]: 101–2.

Chad Hensley, "Kiosk to Kadath," *Spectral Realms* No. 2 (Winter 2015): 96. Reprinted by permission of the author.

Robert E. Howard, "Arkham," *Weird Tales* 20, No. 2 (August 1932): 217.

S. T. Joshi, "To H. P. Lovecraft," *Outré* 2, No. 3 (November 1977): 20. Reprinted by permission of the author.

Rheinhart Kleiner, "At Providence in 1918," *Conservative* 5, No. 1 (July 1919): 8; "Epistle to Mr. and Mrs. Lovecraft," *Brooklynite* 14, No. 2 (April 1924): 1; "The Four of Us!," in Mara Kirk Hart, "Walkers in the City: George Willard Kirk and Howard Phillips Lovecraft in New York City, 1924–1926," *Lovecraft Studies* No. 28 (Spring 1993): 9; "After a Decade," *Californian* 4, No. 2 (Fall 1936): 44; "H. P. L.," *Olympian* No. 35 (Autumn 1940): facing p. 1.

Henry Kuttner, "For H. P. Lovecraft," ms., Wisconsin Historical Society; in H. P. Lovecraft, *Letters to C. L. Moore and Others,* ed. David E. Schultz and S. T. Joshi (New York: Hippocampus Press, 2017), 374; "H. P. L.," *Weird Tales* 30, No. 3 (September 1937): 359. Copyright © 1937 by Henry Kuttner. Reprinted by permission of Don Congdon Associates, Inc.

Lilith Lorraine, "The Acolytes," *Acolyte* 4, No. 2 (Spring 1946): 11.

Frank Belknap Long, "[To Lewis Theobald]," included in a letter to HPL (23 December 1925; ms., John Hay Library, Brown University). "H. P. Lovecraft," *Weird Tales* 31, No. 6 (June 1938): 683.

Charles Lovecraft, "Azathoth." *Spectral Realms* No. 3 (Summer 2015): 78; "The King of Horrors, Howard Phillips Lovecraft" *Spectral Realm* No. 8 (Winter 2018): 49–51; "O Iranon." *Spectral Realms* No. 13 (Summer 2020): 43.

Samuel Loveman, "To Satan," *Conservative* No. 13 (July 1923): 1–2; "Bacchanale," *United Amateur* 23, No. 1 (May 1924): 1; "To Mr. Theobald," *United Amateur* 25, No. 3 (July 1926): 8.

Robert A. W. Lowndes, "For Howard Phillips Lovecraft." *Famous Fantastic Mysteries* 3, No. 4 (October 1941): 115.

Richard Ely Morse, "Mad Dream," *Californian* 4, No. 2 (Fall 1936): 39; "In Memoriam: H. P. Lovecraft," in H. P. Lovecraft et al., *Marginalia,* ed. August Derleth and Donald Wandrei (Sauk City, WI: Arkham House, 1944), 376–77.

Ngo Binh Anh Khoa, "The Sunken City." Previously unpublished. Printed by permission of the author.

Manuel Pérez-Campos, "*Ave Augustissime:* An Acrostic Sonnet on H. P. Lovecraft, Esq.," *Spectral Realms* No. 7 (Summer 2017): 24; "On a Threadbare Photograph of H. P. L. at 66 College St.," *Spectral Realms* No. 11 (Summer 2019): 15; "Stanzas of the Metaphysical Student Found in a Notebook," *Spectral Realms* No. 8 (Winter 2018): 80–81. Reprinted by permission of the author.

Emil Petaja, "Lost Dream," *Weird Tales* 31, No. 1 (January 1938): 96.

Fred Phillips, "Lovecraft." Previously unpublished. Printed by permission of the author. "Shadow over Arkham," in Phillips's *Winds from Sheol* (New York, Hippocampus Press, 2017), 15. Reprinted by permission of the author.

W. H. Pugmire, "'The Hound,'" *Spectral Realms* No. 1 (Summer 2014): 84; "'The Outsider,'" *Spectral Realms* No. 2 (Winter 2015): 63. Reprinted by permission of the Estate of W. H. Pugmire.

Brett Rutherford, "At Lovecraft's Grave," *Lovecraft Studies* No. 15 (Fall 1987): 59–64. Reprinted by permission of the author.

John Milton Samples, "A Greeting," *Silver Clarion* 2, No. 11 (February 1919): 5.

Frank Earle Schermerhorn, "Yet Still We Mourn," *Californian* 5, No. 3 (Summer 1937): 9.

Ann K. Schwader, "In Memoriam Arthur Jermyn," in Schwader's *The Worms Remember* (Griffin, IN: Hive Press, 2001), 54; "The Coming of Chaos," in *The Worms Remember*, 23; "Faint Echoes," in Schwader's *Twisted in Dream* (New York: Hippocampus Press, 2011), 62–63. Reprinted by permission of the author. "Sentinel Hill" (with David C.

Kopaska-Merkel). Previously unpublished. Printed by permission of the authors.

Darrell Schweitzer, "Dancing Before Azathoth," *Spectral Realms* No. 14 (Winter 2021): 92–93. Reprinted by permission of the author.

J. Vernon Shea, "A Walk in Providence," in Shea's *In Search of Lovecraft* (Necronomicon Press, 1991).

Clark Ashton Smith, "To Howard Phillips Lovecraft," *Weird Tales* 30, No. 1 (July 1937): 48; "H. P. L.," in H. P. Lovecraft et al., *The Shuttered Room and Other Pieces,* ed. August Derleth (Sauk City, WI: Arkham House, 1959), 204. Reprinted by permission of the Estate of Clark Ashton Smith.

Vincent Starrett, "HPL," in H. P. Lovecraft et al., *Something about Cats and Other Pieces,* ed. August Derleth (Sauk City, WI: Arkham House, 1949), 306.

Felix Stefanile, "Homage to H. P. Lovecraft," in H. P. Lovecraft et al., *The Shuttered Room and Other Pieces,* ed. August Derleth (Sauk City, WI: Arkham House, 1959), 202–3.

Richard L. Tierney, "Mountains of Madness," *Macabre* No. 14 (Winter 1963/64): 22; "To Great Cthulhu," *Arkham Collector* No. 9 (Spring 1971): 258. Reprinted by permission of the Estate of Richard L. Tierney.

Elizabeth Toldridge, "H. P. Lovecraft," *Leaves* No. 1 (Summer 1937): 63; "Divinity," in H. P. Lovecraft, *Letters to Elizabeth Toldridge and Anne Tillery Renshaw,* ed. David E. Schultz and S. T. Joshi (New York: Hippocampus Press, 2014), 398.

DJ Tyrer, "Things Man Was Meant to Know." Previously unpublished. Printed by permission of the author.

Donald Wandrei, "The Unknown Color," in Wandrei's *Poems for Midnight* (Sauk City, WI: Arkham House, 1964), 58. Reprinted by permission of the Estate of Harold Hughesdon.

Robert H. Waugh, "In Swan Point Cemetery," in Waugh's *A Monster of Voices: Speaking for H. P. Lovecraft* (New York: Hippocampus Press, 2011), 369–70. Reprinted by permission of the author.

M. F. Webb, "The Keeper of the Innsmouth Light," *Spectral Realms* No. 2 (Winter 2015): 76–77; "Forty Years in Innsmouth," *Spectral Realms* No. 3 (Summer 2018): 18–19. Reprinted by permission of the author.

Henry George Weiss, "To Howard Phillips Lovecraft," *Weird Tales* 31, No. 3 (May 1938): 361 (as by "Francis Flagg").

Andrew White, "Lovecraftian Visions: A Grander Species of Monster." Previously unpublished. Printed by permission of the author.

Charles E. White, "For the Outsider: H. P. Lovecraft," in H. P. Lovecraft et al., *Marginalia*, ed. August Derleth and Donald Wandrei (Sauk City, WI: Arkham House, 1944), 375–76.

About the Contributors

Virginia Anderson (née Virginia Combs; 1920–1987) was born in Crandon, Wisconsin, and spent much of her career writing for the *Southside Urban News Sun* (Milwaukee). She published a story and several poems in the *Acolyte,* and one poem in *Famous Fantastic Mysteries.* For some of these works she used the pseudonym "Nanek," borrowed from the Sikh religion—Guru Nanak was the founder of Sikhism.

Manuel Arenas is a writer of verse and prose in the Gothic horror tradition. His work has appeared in *Spectral Realms* and *Penumbra,* both from Hippocampus Press, and in sundry genre anthologies. In 2021 he released his first collection of prose and poetry, *Book of Shadows: Grim Tales and Gothic Fancies,* from Jackanapes Press.

Ross Balcom lives in Southern California. His poems have appeared in *Beyond Centauri, inkscrawl, Poetry Midwest, Scifaikuest, Star*Line,* and other publications. He is a frequent contributor to *Songs of Eretz Poetry Review.*

David Barker has been writing supernatural fiction and poetry since the mid-1980s. In collaboration with the late W. H. Pugmire, he wrote three books of Lovecraftian fiction: *The Revenant of Rebecca Pascal* (2014), *In the Gulfs of Dream and Other Lovecraftian Tales* (2015), and *Witches in Dreamland* (2018), all three of which will be published in German language editions. David's collection of horror stories *Her Wan Embrace* was published in 2022. He lives in Oregon with his wife, Judy.

R. H. Barlow (1918–1951), author and collector. As a teenager he corresponded with Lovecraft and acted as his host during two long visits in the summers of 1934 and 1935. In the 1930s he wrote several works of weird and fantasy fiction, some in collaboration with Lovecraft. He established the Dragon-Fly Press. Lovecraft appointed him his literary executor, and he assisted August Derleth and Donald Wandrei in preparing the early Lovecraft volumes for Arkham House. In the 1940s he went to Mexico and became a distinguished anthropologist. His fiction, poetry, and essays are gathered in *Eyes of the God* (2022).

F. J. Bergmann (pseudonym of Jeannie Bergmann) is an American editor and writer of speculative poetry and prose fiction. She edits poetry for *Mobius: The Journal of Social Change* and imagines tragedies on or near exoplanets. His work appears irregularly in *Analog, Asimov's, Polu Texni, Pulp Literature, Silver Blade,* and elsewhere. *A Catalogue of the Further Suns,* a collection of dystopian first-contact poems, won the 2017 Gold Line Press poetry chapbook contest and is available at fibitz.com.

Rhysling and Australian Shadows Awards-nominated poet **Leigh Blackmore** debuted in weird verse with a Lovecraftian sonnet published in R. Alain Everts's journal, the *Arkham Sampler* (new series, 1984). His fantastic poetry has been widely published since in magazines and anthologies. Representative samples can be found in *Spores from Sharnoth and Other Madnesses* (2008) and its variant spinoff, *Sharnoth's Spores and Other Seeds* (2010). A third weird verse collection, *Azathoth and Other Horrors by Edward Pickman Derby,* along with a weird fiction collection, *Nightmare Logic,* are both forthcoming from IFGW Publishing Australia.

Adam Bolivar is a poet of dark fantasy, a weird fiction writer, and a marionette playwright. He is the author of *The Lay of Old Hex* (Hippocampus Press, 2017), *The Ettinfell of Beacon Hill* (Jackanapes Press, 2021), *Ballads for the Witching Hour* (Hippocampus Press 2022), and *A Wheel of Ravens* (Jackanapes Press, 2023). A native of Boston, he now resides in Portland, Oregon.

Joseph Payne Brennan (1918–1990) was an American writer of fantasy and horror fiction, and also a poet. He edited the magazines *Macabre* (1957–1976) and *Essence* (1950–1977). His first book of verse was *Heart of Earth* 1950). Others include *Sixty Selected Poems* (1985) and *Look Back on Laurel Hills* (1989).

Albert Chapin (1869–1946) was the editor and publisher of the amateur journal *The Minstrel.*

Formalist speculative poet **Frank Coffman** is a retired professor of English, Creative Writing, and Journalism. He has published speculative poetry and fiction in a variety of journals, magazines, anthologies, and collections. His three large poetry collections are: *The Coven's Hornbook & Other Poems* (2019), *Black Flames & Gleaming Shadows* (2020), and *Eclipse of the Moon* (2021). His first fiction collection, *Three against the Dark: Collected Dr. Venn Occult Detective Mysteries,* was published in March 2022.

Scott J. Couturier is a Rhysling Award-nominated poet and prose writer of the weird, liminal, and darkly fantastic. His work has appeared in numerous venues, including *The Audient Void, Spectral Realms, The Dark Corner Zine, Space & Time,* and *Weirdbook.* Currently he works as a copy and content editor for Mission Point Press, living an obscure reverie in the wilds of northern Michigan with his partner/live-in editor and two cats. His collection of weird fiction *The Box* was released in June 2022 by Hybrid Sequence Media, and his collection of weird and autumnal verse, *I Awaken in October,* appeared in 2022 from Jackanapes Press.

August Derleth (1909–1971) was an author of weird tales and also a long series of regional and historical works set in his native Wisconsin. After Lovecraft's death, he and Donald Wandrei founded Arkham House to preserve Lovecraft's work in book form. See *Essential Solitude* for his correspondence with Lovecraft. He published numerous volumes of poetry, much of it gathered in *Collected Poems* (1967).

Linn Donlon is a middle-aged research scientist from a flyover state whose coworkers have been hoodwinked into thinking she is fairly normal. Most of her publications are effective cures for insomnia. She is currently owned by two cats, one feral and one sessile, and spends her leisure time opening cans.

Ian Futter began writing stories and poems in his childhood, but only lately has started to share them. His poems have appeared in *The Darke Phantastique* and *Spectral Realms.* He continues to produce dark fiction for admirers of the surreal.

Alfred Galpin (1901–1983) was an amateur journalist and correspondent of Lovecraft. He studied music in Paris and was also a scholar in French literature. For Lovecraft's letters to him, see *Letters to Alfred Galpin and Others* (2020).

Wade German's most recent full-length poetry collection is *Psalms and Sorceries* (Hippocampus Press, 2022). His first collection, *Dreams from a Black Nebula* (2014) is also available from Hippocampus Press. Other titles include four slim volumes of his selected poems with Portuguese translation: *Incantations, Apparitions, Phantasmagorias,* and the latest, *Chapel of Celluloid* (Raphus Press, 2023).

Maxwell I. Gold is an author of weird fiction and dark fantasy. His work has been published in *Spectral Realms, The Audient Void, Hinnom Magazine,* and elsewhere. His short story "A Credible Fear" appeared in *The Offbeat,* the literary journal of Michigan State University's Department of Creative Writing and Rhetoric. He studied philosophy and political science at the University of Toledo and is an active member of the Horror Writers Association.

Arthur Goodenough (1871–1936) was an amateur poet who resided in Brattleboro, Vermont. Lovecraft visited him there on several occasions. He is the author of *Songs of Four Decades* (W. Paul Cook, 1927).

Chad Hensley's most recent book of horror poetry, *Embrace the Hideous Immaculate,* is available from Raw Dog Screaming Press. His recent poetry appearances include *Spectral Realms, Weirdbook,* and *Skelos.* Hensley is also a crafted reporter on cultural extremes in music and art, seeing several years of his writing on underground subjects published in the book *EsoTerra: The Journal of Extreme Culture* (Creation Books). Hensley's most recent horror fiction has appeared in *Weirdbook Annual: Zombies!* and *Weirdbook* #39.

Robert E. Howard (1906–1936) was a prolific Texas author of weird and adventure tales for *Weird Tales* and other pulp magazines; he was the creator of the adventure hero Conan the Cimmerian. He and Lovecraft corresponded voluminously from 1930 to 1936. See *A Means to Freedom* (2009) for his correspondence with Lovecraft. His poems are collected a three-volume edition published by Robert E. Howard Foundation Press (2022–23).

S. T. Joshi is a leading authority on H. P. Lovecraft and has edited his collected fiction, poetry, essays, and letters, in addition to writing *I Am Providence: The Life and Times of H. P. Lovecraft* (2010) and other critical and biographical works on Lovecraft and other authors of weird fiction.

Rheinhart Kleiner (1892–1947), an amateur journalist, was one of Lovecraft's earliest correspondents. His poetry collections include *Pegasus in Pasture.* Lovecraft's letters to him are published in *Letters to Rheinhart Kleiner and Others* (2020). The volume includes numerous poems by Kleiner, as well as his memoirs of Lovecraft.

Ngo Binh Anh Khoa is a teacher of English in Ho Chi Minh City, Vietnam. In his free time, he enjoys reading fiction and writing speculative poetry, some of which have appeared in *Weirdbook, Star*Line, Spectral Realms, The Audient Void,* and other venues.

David C. Kopaska-Merkel has been writing speculative poetry and fiction since the 1970s. He won the 2006 Rhysling Award for best long poem (for a collaboration with Kendall Evans), and edits *Dreams & Nightmares* magazine (since 1986). He has served as SFPA president and is an SFPA Grandmaster. His poems (more than 1200) have been published in *Asimov's*, *Strange Horizons*, and more than 200 other venues. *Some Disassembly Required*, his latest collection of dark poetry, was published by Diminuendo Press in 2022.

Henry Kuttner (1915–1958), prolific American author of science fiction, fantasy and horror. Lovecraft's letters to him are published in *Letters to C. L. Moore and Others* (2017).

Lilith Lorraine (pseudonym of Mary Maude Wright [née Dunn]; 1894–1967) was an associate of Clark Ashton Smith and was a widely published poet in pulp and fan magazines. She published the poetry collection *Wine of Wonder* (1952) and the poetry anthology *Tomorrow's Conquerors* (1947).

Frank Belknap Long (1901–1994), fiction writer and poet and one of Lovecraft's closest friends and correspondents. Late in life he wrote the memoir *Howard Phillips Lovecraft: Dreamer on the Nightside* (1975). Long's poetry volumes include *A Man from Genoa* (W. Paul Cook, 1926), *The Goblin Tower* (Dragon-Fly Press, 1935), and *In Mayan Splendor* (Arkham House, 1977).

Charles Lovecraft is an Australian writer, editor, and publisher of P'rea Press (www.preapress.com) specializing in fantasy and supernatural poetry, fiction, nonfiction, and Australian and international authors. His favorite authors and greatest influences are H. P. Lovecraft, Shakespeare, Shelley, Keats, Clark Ashton Smith, George Sterling, and Richard L. Tierney. Charles has published more than 150 poems and essays of fantasy and has edited and published more than 40 books.

Samuel Loveman (1887–1976), poet and longtime friend of Lovecraft and Donald Wandrei as well as of Ambrose Bierce, Hart Crane, George Sterling, and Clark Ashton Smith. He wrote *The Hermaphrodite* (1926) and other works. See *Letters to Alfred Galpin and Others* (2020) for a few surviving letters to him by Lovecraft. His poetry, fiction, and essays are gathered in *Out of the Immortal Night* (2021).

Robert A. W. Lowndes (1916–1998) was a prolific editor and publisher of weird and science fiction digest magazines, including *Magazine of Horror* and *Bizarre Fantasy Tales.* He wrote several science fiction novels as well as the nonfiction volume *Three Faces of Science Fiction* (1973). Lovecraft's two letters to him are included in *Miscellaneous Letters* (2022).

Richard Ely Morse (1909–1986) was a poet, librarian, and late correspondent of Lovecraft. He was the author of *Winter Garden* (Poetry Society of Amherst College, 1931). Many of his poems and Lovecraft's letters to him are published in *Letters to Hyman Bradofsky and Others* (2023).

Manuel Pérez-Campos of Bayamón, Puerto Rico, is a longtime poet in the tradition of the weird. His poetry has appeared previously in *Spectral Realms* and *Weird Fiction Review.*

Emil Petaja (1915–2000) was an American science fiction and fantasy writer whose career spanned seven decades. His letters from Lovecraft are published in *Letters with Donald and Howard Wandrei and to Emil Petaja* (2019).

Fred Phillips has been published in the *Cimmerian, Studies in the Fantastic, Weird Fiction Review,* and elsewhere. His first collection of poetry, *From the Cauldron,* was published by Hippocampus Press in 2010. A second collection, *Winds from Sheol,* appeared in 2017.

W. H. Pugmire (1951–2019) was a writer of weird fiction and horror fiction based in Seattle. *Uncommon Places: A Collection of Exquisites* (Hippocampus Press, 2012) is a book of prose poems, while *Some Unknown Gulf of Night* (Arcane Wisdom, 2011) is a skillful rewriting of Lovecraft's *Fungi from Yuggoth* into prose vignettes.

Brett Rutherford has published 18 volumes of poetry, two novels, and over 600 magazine articles, monographs and studies. He founded The Poet's Press in New York City, and has published 300 books to date, with work from almost 400 authors. In retirement, he now composes music. He is the author of *Trilobite Love Song: Selected Poems & Revisions, 2013–2014* (The Poet's Press, 2014).

John Milton Samples (1887–1944) of Macon, Georgia (later Atlanta), was an amateur journalist and editor of the *Silver Clarion,* to which Lovecraft contributed a few poems. His verse appeared in *Visions in Verse* (1912).

Frank Earle Schermerhorn (1870–1957) was a member of the Philadelphia bar. His verse appeared in *Invisible and Other Poems* (1956). He was also the author of *American and French Flags of the Revolution, 1775–1783* (1948).

Ann K. Schwader lives and writes in Colorado. Her most recent collection, *Unquiet Stars* (2021), is now out from Weird House Press. Two of her earlier collections, *Wild Hunt of the Stars* (Sam's Dot, 2010) and *Dark Energies* (P'rea Press, 2015), were Bram Stoker Award finalists. In 2018, she received the Science Fiction & Fantasy Poetry Association's Grand Master award. She is also a two-time Rhysling Award winner. *Twisted in Dream* (Hippocampus Press, 2011) is a volume of her collected weird verse.

Darrell Schweitzer is a short story writer and novelist, and former coeditor of *Weird Tales.* He has published much humorous Lovecraftian verse, such as *Non Compost Mentis* (Zadok Allen, 1993), and also has two serious poetry collections in print, *Groping Toward the Light* (Wildside Press, 2000) and *Ghosts of Past and Future* (Wildside Press, 2008).

J. Vernon Shea (1912–1981) was a young cinema and weird fiction fan from Pittsburgh who began corresponding with Lovecraft in 1931. For Lovecraft's letters to him, see *Letters to J. Vernon Shea, Carl F. Strauch, and Lee McBride White* (2016).

Clark Ashton Smith (1893–1961) was a prolific California poet and writer of fantasy tales. He is the author of *The Star-Treader and Other Poems* (1912), *Ebony and Crystal* (1922), *Sandalwood* (1925), *The Dark Chateau* (1951), and *Spells and Philtres* (1958). He received a "fan" letter from Lovecraft in 1922 and corresponded with him until Lovecraft's death. Their joint correspondence is contained in *Dawnward Spire, Lonely Hill* (2017). His verse is gathered in *The Complete Poetry and Translations of Clark Ashton Smith* (three volumes, 2007–08).

Vincent Starrett (1886–1974) was an American bookman who corresponded briefly with Lovecraft in 1927. See *Letters to Maurice W. Moe and Others* (2018) for Lovecraft's letters to him. His poetry volumes include *Autolycus in Limbo* (E. P. Dutton, 1943).

For forty-six years (1954–2000), **Felix Stefanile** (1920–2009) and his wife Selma edited and published the poetry magazine *Sparrow*. *Songs of the Sparrow: The Poetry of Felix Stefanile* (Bordighera Press, 2015) reproduces his seven collections, from *River Full of Craft* (1956) to *The Country of Absence* (2000). He also published three volumes of verse translation.

Richard L. Tierney's (1936–2022) *Collected Poems* appeared from Arkham House in 1981. A later volume of poetry was published as *Savage Menace and Other Poems of Horror* (P'rea Press, 2010). Tierney is also the author of *The Winds of Zarr* (Silver Scarab Press, 1975), *The House of the Toad* (Fedogan & Bremer, 1993), and many other works of horror and fantasy fiction.

Elizabeth Toldridge (1861–1940) was a poet living in Washington, D.C., who corresponded with Lovecraft from 1928 to 1937. She was the author of *Mother's Love Songs* (Boston: Richard Badger/Gorham Press, 1911) and *The Soul of Love* (New York: Broadway Pub. Co., 1910). Lovecraft's letters to her and a selection of her verse are published in *Letters to Elizabeth Toldridge and Anne Tillery Renshaw* (2014).

DJ Tyrer is the person behind Atlantean Publishing and has been published in *The Rhysling Anthology*, issues of *Cyäegha*, *The Horrorzine*, *Scifaikuest*, *Sirens Call*, *Star*Line*, *Tigershark*, and The *Yellow Zine*. The echapbook *One Vision* is available from Tigershark Publishing. *SuperTrump* and *A Wuhan Whodunnit* are available for download from Atlantean Publishing.

Donald Wandrei (1908–1987) was a poet and author of weird fiction, science fiction, and detective tales. His first published books were poetry: *Ecstasy* (1928) and *Dark Odyssey* (1931). He corresponded with Lovecraft from 1926 to 1937, visited Lovecraft in Providence in 1927 and 1932, and met Lovecraft occasionally in New York during the 1930s. For their joint correspondence, see *H. P. Lovecraft: Letters with Donald and Howard Wandrei and to Emil Petaja* (2019). His *Sonnets of the Midnight Hours* had a profound effect on Lovecraft's composition of *Fungi from Yuggoth* (1929–30). After Lovecraft's death he and August Derleth founded the publishing firm Arkham House to preserve Lovecraft's work. His poetry is gathered in *Sanctity and Sin: The Collected Poems and Prose Poems* (Hippocampus Press, 2008).

Robert H. Waugh is the author of three volumes of critical essays on Lovecraft: *The Monster in the Mirror* (2006), *A Monster of Voices* (2011), and *A Monster for Many* (2021). He has also edited the critical anthology *Lovecraft and Influence* (2013) and authored the critical study *The Tragic Thread in Science Fiction* (2019).

M. F. Webb's poetry has appeared in *Spectral Realms*, and her fiction has been published in *Latchkey Tales*. She hails from a Victorian seaport town in Washington State.

Henry George Weiss (1898–1946) was an American poet, writer and novelist. His science fiction stories and poetry appeared under the pseudonym "Francis Flagg" in *Amazing Stories*, *Astounding*, *Driftwind*, *Fantasy Magazine*, *Leaves*, *Tales of Wonder*, *Weird Tales*, and elsewhere.

Andrew White is an aspiring writer who lives like a monk in the mountains of North Carolina. He is inspired by metal music, mythology, mysticism and all things Gothic/Lovecraftian. Andrew loves nature, his family, and his books. He tries not to take himself too seriously.

Charles E. White (1908–1977) of Attleboro, Massachusetts, corresponded with August Derleth in the 1940s. Derleth published his poem "For the Outsider" in *Marginalia* (1944).

Indexes

Authors

Titles and First Lines

www.ingramcontent.com/pod-product-compliance
Lightning Source LLC
LaVergne TN
LVHW050645100826
845148LV00011B/1991

* 9 7 8 1 6 1 4 9 8 4 1 3 9 *